40 YEARS OF

BREATHING

40 YEARS OF BREATHING

A Personal Journey through Yoga, Judaism and Our Natural World

Linda A. Roe

authorHOUSE®

AuthorHouse™
1663 Liberty Drive
Bloomington, IN 47403
www.authorhouse.com
Phone: 1-800-839-8640

First published by AuthorHouse   07/09/2011

ISBN: 978-1-4634-1022-3 (sc)
ISBN: 978-1-4634-1021-6 (ebk)

Library of Congress Control Number: 2011908959

Printed in the United States of America

Any people depicted in stock imagery provided by Thinkstock are models, and such images are being used for illustrative purposes only.
Certain stock imagery © Thinkstock.

This book is printed on acid-free paper.

Prologue

I am a chaplain and in chaplaincy, we would say that this book is my Theory of Ministry. It came out of me organically, and is the integration of my philosophy of Judaism, Science and Yoga. There are some wild ideas in this book and that's OK with me. In my heart I am a very wild person.

I was sustained and encouraged by several people while I was writing this book. Melody Madonna and Joe Hutchinson—thank you very much for reading each of these articles as soon as I wrote them. Thank you to my friend-from-birth Beth Beery. Great growing up with you, great growing old with you—and because we are by no means old yet I look forward to many more years with you. My yoga teachers Nancy Stechert and Jayne Satter are always a joy. My rabbi Adam Morris—it sure is a pleasure watching you and experiencing you as a rabbi. And to the love of my life, Darice, I say, "Wow!" You're the greatest.

Breathing

The first time I wondered why I was breathing was when I was two years old. I noticed that air was going in and out of my nose and I didn't know why. I tried not breathing and found that wasn't possible, but I couldn't understand why breathing was necessary. Figuring out why I needed to eat and drink was easier—to the two-year-old mind it was obvious, but I couldn't understand breathing. That need to comprehend breathing has stayed with me—and now 40 years later, I'm finally beginning to answer my question.

Judaism is a religion that I love. It is a part of my being—in ways that I am still only beginning to understand. As I have changed, the parts of Judaism that speak to me have changed too. A good example of this is the Sh'ma. This most important prayer/meditation has never meant very much to me—even though I know that it expresses a lot of what it means to be a Jew. I say it along with everybody else when I'm at services, but have never really put my energy into it. However, now that I'm seeing more about why we breathe, I'm also seeing more in this watchword of Judaism. *Sh'ma Yisrael, Adonai Eloheinu, Adonai Echad.* Listen Up Israel! Hashem is our God and our God is ONE!

Webster's Ninth Collegiate Dictionary says that ONE is the number denoting UNITY. It goes on to say that ONE constitutes a unified entity of two or more components. The verb unify indicates a process of becoming ONE. But if God is already ONE, then where is the process? Where are the two or more components that are becoming ONE? We find the answer by understanding breathing.

Judaism says that God created the world by speaking. The first thing that God spoke about was Light. On that first day of creation, we see three things—Breath, Light, and then the absence of Light, or Darkness. Looking a little closer, we can see a fourth—Movement.

Breath is all about Movement. There is the In-Breath and there is the Out-Breath. But Light is also about movement because we can only have Light if we have Darkness—so we move from Darkness into Light and from Light into Darkness. The linking together of Light and Darkness through Movement means that we can participate in the process of UNITY. Another way of saying this is—Breath creates Light and Breath creates Darkness through Movement. Everything is linked and it is the linking which is the KEY.

One of my favorite things to do is to sing a *niggun*. I love singing a niggun on Friday night to begin Shabbat dinner or to link hand washing with *motzi*. The niggun, because it repeats itself over and over is said to peel away the layers of a person and allows a person to reach the very core of their being. Why does singing have the power to do that? Because when we use our breath to sing we are actually connecting with the other layers of our being. To understand this, we need to look closely at the layers of the body.

Yoga speaks very clearly about the layers of a Human Being. <u>The Tibetan Book of Yoga</u> says there are 5 different layers. These layers are:

1. The layer of the physical body
2. The layer that sustains the physical body
3. The layer of communication within the body
4. The layer of thought
5. The layer of the mind

<u>The Tibetan Book of Yoga</u> describes each of those layers in detail, saying that in the second layer lies anything that gives sustenance to the body. Food and water, as well as breathing are located in the second layer. But breathing is so very much more important than eating or drinking and we must cut ourselves off from breathing when we eat or drink that I am going to describe the second layer simply as Breath. The third layer contains the Central Nervous System, which is where the electrical system of our body is. Looking at the layers in this way gives us another way to describe them.

1. Physical body
2. Breath
3. Light
4. Movement
5. Stillness

All of the layers are linked. This means that making changes in the physical body or the Breath will make changes in the amount of Light, the amount of Movement (thoughts) and the amount of Stillness (Mind) available to us.

So far we have looked only at the layer of Breath, saying there is the In-Breath and the Out-Breath. <u>The Tibetan Book of Yoga</u> says that life begins with an initial In-Breath at birth, and ends with a final Out-Breath at the moment of death. We can see this when we look at a tombstone as well. Tombstones frequently have two dates on them separated by a hyphen: Birth, Death and the Space in between—or, the first In-Breath, the last Out-Breath and the Space in between. We all know that everything we are takes place in the Space of the hyphen—the Space in between. This means that we must look more closely at Space.

What do Judaism and Yoga have to say about Space? Both say that Space is very important and both say that creating Space is not trivial. The Jews were made to wander in the desert for 40 years before they were allowed into their Holy Land (Holy Space). Yoga tries to create space regardless of what is happening in the outside world. No matter how the body is bent or twisted, the goal is to create space. Creating space helps us to find our Center and finding our Center allows us to remain non-violent both to ourselves and others. We learn to support the heart by creating space in the body, and in that way our heart can open up to All.

Before the universe was created, God was All there was. Because God's essence was All, there was no Space to create anything. In order to Create, God pulled some of the essence back—*tsimtsum*—and put some of that essence into physical form. In other words, God's Light took on a physical form in order to create the universe. This means that each person has God's Light within—in the form of Divine Sparks.

Looking a little closer at tsimtsum we can see that it describes God's initial breath. The pulling back is the In-Breath (creating Space) and then the world was created through the Out-Breath, but it was a controlled Out-Breath (why we must also learn to control our breath), leaving everything in the universe permeated with God's essence or Light. And here's the interesting part—liberating the Divine Light—or Divine Sparks as they are commonly referred to actually increases the intensity of Divine Light available to the universe!

Where can we find Divine Sparks most easily in our body? To answer that question we return to Webster's Ninth Collegiate Dictionary. There, a spark is described as "a luminous disruptive electrical discharge of very short duration between two conductors separated by a gas (as air)." This is very interesting because we have such a space within our body—in the Central Nervous System. In the gap between two neurons, a spark travels when a message needs to get somewhere in the body. This means that God is in the Spaces. Looking in this way at Space we see that God was with the Jews when they were traveling in the Space of the desert, and when they were finally allowed into their Holy Land and we see that God is present with us each time we breathe. How nice to know that since we are constantly breathing, God is constantly with us. And since our lives can be described so easily as the Space between the two dates on our tombstone, it is another way to see that God is always with us. Now we understand that we breathe in order to create Space, and we create Space to find God. We find God to find ourselves and what we're really doing is breathing in order to become ONE. The reassuring part for me is that since we can't help but breathe, we can't help but become ONE.

I once described yoga to a friend by saying that it justified my body and soul. It was the best way to describe how I felt after a yoga class because the word justify has a very physical meaning to me. Some time ago I worked at a book publisher where my job was to put books together. When all of the pages had been cut and ordered, I would pick up the stack of papers and hold them edgewise between my two hands and then bang the papers up and down on a table. This was called justifying the book and I loved doing it, although the process could be quite painful. Quite frequently I received nasty paper cuts and a couple of times I saw books that were actually soaked in blood. But the pain was outweighed by the absolute pleasure of holding a stack of papers that had been transformed into something whole—a unit—a book. In many ways, I am that new book after a yoga class. All of my edges have been put back into order and I am once again complete.

Open Places

I wonder what exactly is happening with yoga. I have spent the majority of my life doing every sport I can get my hands on—why haven't I felt transformed before?

Even though I am not yet completely sure of the difference between yoga and exercise, I know that my focus is inwards in yoga and outwards in exercise. I once played soccer against a team that was ranked second in the nation. Playing them was very exciting for me and although my team lost decisively, I had a great time. Part way into the second half of the game my best friend came over and asked why I was being such a bitch. I asked her what she meant and she said, "You're guarding me and haven't spoken one word to me." I was completely confused because Amy was on MY team—how could I be guarding her? But at halftime our teams had switched players—mostly because they were beating us so badly. Amy had gone over to the other team and had become their center forward. I had been going all over the field, sticking very close to Amy, but my focus had been on the space between Amy and the ball. I had noticed that I was probably guarding a new person, because I could see the silhouette of Amy's frizzy hair in my peripheral vision, and I was certainly enjoying Amy's soccer skill, but I wasn't focusing on her as a human being—I was intent on following her only in relation to the position of the ball on the field.

Yoga is different. There's nothing to defend against, nothing to "do" really. The only thing is listening to the teacher and seeing where my body is and monitoring how I am feeling. That is it. The amazing thing is that simply by doing those things; I have been carried along in yoga. It is almost as if I put myself in a river and am being carried along with the current.

I have felt this way before. When I spend a lot of time singing in Hebrew, I feel the same way I do in a yoga class. I feel like the Hebrew letters are rungs in a ladder and I am climbing the ladder to God. This is a very real sensation to me. Sometimes I feel like the Hebrew letters are a magic carpet and I am riding the magic carpet to new and interesting places. I have seen people want to stop during services—they want to know the meaning of the words they are saying. But I feel like I just fell off the ladder whenever someone asks the meaning of a prayer during services. I certainly don't mind studying the meaning, but that should come at a different time than during services. When I sing in Hebrew, I am flowing along in a river. If I'm busy wondering about the meaning of the words, then I am watching the flow of the river from the sidelines. When I am in a yoga class, the *asanas* are just like the Hebrew letters for me. So at the beginning of a yoga class, I climb aboard the asanas and see where they take me.

I can see even more similarities when I look at the Hebrew letters and the asanas. Hebrew is a sacred language and all of the letters have meanings. It is said that if a person doesn't know the prayers, they can simply recite the *alef-bet* and God will assemble the prayers for them. This is exactly what happens to me in yoga class. Even though I don't know how to properly do the asanas, I just do them and God puts everything together for me.

When I look at letters I see bent lines. When I look at asanas I also bent lines. This means that I can look more deeply into the letters and see what they can tell me about the asanas. When a person learns Hebrew after having learned a language like English first, they are in for quite a shock. Hebrew is typically written using only consonants. If vowels are to be used, they are simply added in later—as dots either above or below the consonants.

I looked up the meaning of consonant in the Webster's Ninth Collegiate Dictionary and written there was the following:

> One of a class of speech sounds characterized by constriction or closure at one or more points in the breath channel.

I then went to the definition of vowel and I found the following:

> One of a class of speech sounds in the articulation of which the oral part of the breath channel is not blocked and is not constricted enough to cause audible friction.

Hmm . . . Very interesting. It is possible to write an entire language using only consonants, but it is impossible to write more than a couple of words with absolutely no consonants. Constrictions are much more valuable than are the open places! Not that you would be able to guess that from how much we complain about constrictions. And when you think about it, we certainly use a lot of our open places to scream about our constrictions. But sometimes it takes the absence of a constriction to see its importance.

I was born with a dislocated hip. The top of my right femur was not connected to anything. This meant that moving my right leg was problematic, since in order to move, connection to something else is necessary. The hip joint is meant to hold the leg bone and orient it. Without that orientation, the leg doesn't know quite where it should be and as a result ends up being "all over the place." Congenital hip dislocations tend to cause a lot of damage. It is that way in our life as well, but it can be difficult to recognize our constrictions as places that we should be grateful for.

In saying that constrictions are important, it is essential to understand the relationship between our closed places and our open places. We can see this by going back to Hebrew for a minute. When Hebrew is written with vowels it is called "pointed." This means that when we bring our concentration or our focus or to a point, we should be using our open places to do it. If we focus on our constrictions we will end up not moving anywhere because we are facing in the wrong direction. Let me explain.

Our constrictions are meant to orient us and help us move. But quite often we hold on to our constrictions. When we do this we end up facing our past, not our future. I see this important relationship between constrictions and open places most clearly in the story of Pesach (Passover.) For the early Jews, Egypt was a place of refuge, a place that saved their lives. But over time, Egypt became bitter and finally it became so bitter that the only thing to do was to leave. It's never easy to leave a situation; Moses spent a great deal of time and energy convincing the Jews that leaving was the right thing to do. Even so, it wasn't until all of the first born Egyptians had been killed that the Jews found that they really could leave Egypt. In Hebrew, the word used for Egypt is m*itzrayim*—which really means The Narrow Places. Another word that could be used for mitzrayim is The Birth Canal. The whole experience—from leaving Egypt, to looking at the new Holy Land and reacting with only fear, to spending forty years wandering around in a desert—all of these experiences shaped the Jewish people in such a way that several thousands of years later, it is still this story which completely articulates the formation of the Jewish people into an entity. In other words, the Jewish People was born when they went through their mitzrayim—narrow places—and found themselves in the wide open space of the desert.

Freedom can be very scary. One of my absolutely favorite quotes comes from this part of the story. The Jews have left Egypt—they have left behind death and destruction—there is no going back. They are standing at the edge of the sea, and the very angry Egyptians are coming for them. And someone says to Moses, "Were there not enough graves in Egypt that you brought us out here to die?" My God, how many times have I felt that exact feeling? Every time I think about that quote it makes me laugh. Everything will be OK. Just breathe and everything will be all right. I know that looking back on my own personal mitzrayim, my constricting experiences have shaped me in ways that I never could have imagined at the time. By now I have come to recognize my mitzrayim—and I actually sort of look forward to them because I know that without them I would not be the person I am today, and I'm pretty happy to be who I am.

Days of Change

My grandparents used to live on a farm in southeastern Idaho. I loved being on that farm as I have loved no other place on Earth. My favorite thing on the farm was the orchard. I used to love just to walk amongst the trees. They were placed so evenly and the long grass growing between the trees was absolutely perfect to walk through.

In Hebrew, the word for orchard is *pardes*—and in modern times this word has come to mean paradise. Having spent a lot of time in my grandpa's orchard, I know that paradise is correct. At least it was for me—for my grandfather, I know that the orchard was a lot of work. I loved everything about the orchard—so much so that when my grandparents died, I seriously considered living on the farm and continuing their legacy.

Looking back, I'm glad I didn't end up on the farm. There is nothing in me that is suited for owning a farm. I am afraid of heights, I don't like bugs and I can't fix a tractor to save my life. Instead of living on the farm, I have decided to carry it with me. In every house I have owned, the first thing I have done is to plant fruit trees and raspberry bushes.

Life is change—although change is very hard. The last time I was on my grandparents' farm I knew it would be the last time, and it ripped me apart. To this day, fifteen years after my grandparents' death, I become very emotional when I think about never again being on their farm, never hearing their laughter or seeing their faces.

Why is change so hard?

Looking again at the story of Creation, we see that on the first day God created Breath, Light, Darkness and Movement. We also see that movement is the important link between the other three things. When I look at those four things, I see that movement is the one I understand the least: so I want to take a closer look and see where it takes me.

I used to teach high school math. And while I enjoyed teaching math, I know that it is a very difficult subject. When I started teaching math I had to take a class at the university to make sure I had enough credits to teach it. The first day the professor walked in the door and filled the chalkboard with P's, Q's and arrows and I knew I was in BIG trouble. I would get home and attempt the homework and I would find it was absolutely impossible to do anything. No amount of hard work in the class made up for my lack of understanding. The funny thing is, after I took that class, I found that mathematics opened up for me in completely new ways. It was amazing. I would be up in front of the class teaching, and suddenly new understanding would dawn on me. The P's, Q's and arrows had begun talking to me.

Mathematics is a language—and it is the language of Change. Because it is the language of Change, it is the language of the universe. For that reason, I want to take another look at the story of Creation. The first six days were all about change—total and complete. Looking at one day it is impossible to guess what will happen on the next. For example, from creating Light and Dark on the first day, God created the heavens above and below on the second day. Who could have guessed that would have come next? Only on the seventh day did God rest from Creation.

Jews have long discussed what resting from Creation means. But nothing is written about that day, so it is very difficult to determine exactly what is meant. The discussion of rest led the rabbis to say that on Shabbat we are not to partake in any activity which would have been necessary to build the Temple. I would like to look at these first seven days a little differently.

If we look at the six days of creation as *Days of Change*, and look at the seventh as a *Day with No Change*, we get a very different picture. I used to picture the types of activities that God must have done on the seventh day. How was that first Saturday? Saturday's always have a certain feeling to me, and I wondered if that first Saturday had the same feeling. But I never received any information on the subject. Whenever I would try to picture that first Saturday, nothing would come to mind. I brushed it aside, because I used to think about that first Saturday mostly as a joke—of course I know that it is not literal. But now I'm beginning to realize that nothing coming to mind really was the answer to my musings.

So the act of Creation really means Change; which has been with us since the very beginning and will be with us until the very end. As the one thing that remains constant in our lives, you might think that we would cling to change. Instead we cling to something that has never really been.

Linda A. Roe

Judaism says that God is One and that God made the world in duality. When you think about it, duality is a process of cutting one into two. It turns out that being cut into two terrifies us and we fight it with every fiber of our being—even at the same time that Stillness absolutely bores us. It is very difficult for us to remain still—movement is such a part of our very being. This is possible to see in yoga. There are many asanas, and one reason is that if there was only one pose no one would do yoga. No one.

We can put the asanas into two groups. In one group are the asanas that increase flexibility and in the other are those that increase strength. If we are really to embrace Change, we must understand both flexibility and strength.

For many years I studied karate. I loved it. I especially remember one time my teacher's teacher came to town. He was a bit of a storyteller and I remember many things that he said. One of his stories was exactly about the need for balancing flexibility and strength. He said that when he was learning karate he used to drive many miles to study with a teacher who was near Chicago. Over and over again he used to drive the same road, and at a particular turn, he would admire a huge oak tree that was right beside the road. In his karate practice he would imagine himself to be that big oak tree. And then one time he drove that road right after a very big storm. When he got to that particular turn in the road he saw that his beloved oak tree was lying on its side, felled by the big winds of the storm. Looking at the site, he then noticed a grove of willow trees that were right behind the oak tree. He had never noticed them before, but as he looked at them after the big storm, there they were—just as before the storm. And so, my teacher's teacher said, he then changed his karate practice. Instead of trying to be like the oak tree, he began to become like the willow.

A word that is often used in yoga instead of flexibility is openness. And when we see that yoga prepares us for Change, then using the word openness is a good term. Everyone has a certain capacity for openness and a certain capacity for strength. Too much openness without enough strength leaves a person vulnerable to injuries. We can see this in our daily lives as well.

I have said that Creation is Change. But I know from my own life that I have tried to change myself in ways that were not healthy. How can I tell when change is healthy and when change is unhealthy? How can I balance an openness to change with my own inner strength? This has been one of the hardest things I have had to learn in my life—so hard in fact that I am only now beginning to barely scratch the surface of this lesson.

I'm not sure how old I was when I heard this next story for the first time, but I know that I can't remember a time when it wasn't a part of me. When I was born, I was a girl. My mother was devastated as she had been hoping I would be a boy. She said that all first children should be boys. She was in fact so waiting for a boy that she had not even thought about a girl's name. They had to come up with something quickly when they saw I was a girl. My mom said they just chose Linda.

Now I can see that her belief was absurd, but at the time—especially the first time I heard that story, I felt completely unlovable. And I hated that I was a girl. How could God have been so cruel as to make me so flawed? I despaired because no matter how much I tried, I couldn't make myself be a boy. Eventually I gave up trying to be a boy and instead just squashed all of my femininity. It wasn't very long ago that I finally realized that I absolutely love femininity in other people, and if it wasn't something horrible for them, why did it have to be something horrible for me? That thing which I loved so much in other people was something that I also carried within me—and I could love it in myself just as much.

This is an extreme example of trying to change for other people, but I use it because it is something we do on a daily basis. Somebody says something about how I should be or should not be, and I begin to change myself to accommodate that suggestion.

It is easy to become confused here on Earth. Judaism says that people are created in God's image. That is a wonderful concept until you realize that images are backwards. Look in a mirror and you will see this. If I raise my right hand in the mirror, my image raises her left.

To address this issue we must return to constrictions and open places. As I get older I realize that many of the things that I had thought were constrictions were really my open places. And simply by recognizing them as such, my life has taken off.

When I was a kid I used to watch the art teacher go around the room. She would always come to my place, look at my picture and mumble something like, "That's nice." As I grew older, my pictures didn't change. When I draw a person today, I still draw a person like I drew it when I was in elementary school. I used to be the coordinator of a diagnostic clinic for children and I shared an office with the psychologist. He would always have the children draw a self-portrait and then he would show me the portrait when he was done with the examination. I would tell him what I saw in the child's artwork and he would always dismiss what I said. His thing that he would say about each child seemed to be that the pictures were missing details. I would always squirm a little because quite often these kids had more detail in their pictures than I would. All my life I have been told that I am not a detail person and that I should work on that. Finally, after sharing an office with this very mixed up psychologist, I realized that I would never be a detail person and that would be OK. My artwork would always have no detail to it.

Almost as soon as I made that realization, artwork began popping out of me. None of it had detail, but all of it was beautiful—and it expressed my emotions exactly. I learned a very important lesson from that. Now I listen to what people say to me. I listen to whether they are pointing out something to me that is a constriction—or whether they are pointing out something that is really an open place. Either way, I'm grateful for the information, because it sets me in motion.

Movement

I n one of my many chemistry classes in college I made plastic wrap. I remember this particular lab as one of my favorites—normally I absolutely hated chemistry labs. In this lab, we poured a bunch of chemicals together just like we always did. But this time, two layers formed—two distinct layers, kind of like oil and water. Normally when this happens, my impulse is to stir or shake the two layers together to make a single mixture—sort of like what we do with vinegar and oil. But in order to make plastic wrap, you must do something different—stirring or shaking the two layers together will give you absolutely nothing you can use. Oh there will be a reaction all right, but the reaction will lead to nothing useful. Of course, doing the opposite will also lead to nothing useful. If you were to just let the two layers sit—the one on top of the other—you would notice that a thin film appeared between the two layers, and then nothing else would occur. Well, what is happening? And how do you make what is happening useful?

Our job was to carefully stick a glass rod down into the bottom layer and then draw the glass rod up through the top layer. In doing this, a thin string appeared, coming out of the two layers and attached to the glass rod. By winding this string around the glass rod, it was possible to keep the string going. By the end, when one of the layers had been used up, I had a very long string wound around my glass rod.

I loved this lab for many reasons. First, I had never seen this type of reaction before—a reaction that would occur at the interface between two layers. A reaction that you could control time-wise simply by controlling how much contact was made between the layers. But I also loved this lab because plastic wrap was made by mistake. Some guy just happened to notice that if he stirred everything together all he got was a big clump of goo, but if he reached down deep into the glass, and brought stuff from the bottom to the top, he could make a very strong fiber. And we've all seen the many uses for plastic wrap—anything from covering up your food in the refrigerator to fashioning a fancy dress that your husband may or may not like.

I have been pulling such a string out of me with all of the things I have been writing about. But now I can see that it is time to begin knitting with this string.

In the first article I wrote about the different layers of the body. These were the physical body, the breath, the light, the movement and the layer of stillness. I have spoken about four of the layers, leaving one layer largely untouched.

It is the layer of Stillness which gives me fits. But I also know that everything I need to know or understand about Stillness lies inside of me. I need look nowhere else for it.

The Talmud says that whoever saves a single person saves the entire world. It is here that I begin my quest for Stillness.

One night in April 2006, when I went to Mexico for a yoga retreat, I was out walking along the beach one night thinking about the above statement from the Talmud. Standing on that beach on the Caribbean Ocean, I realized something. What I was seeing outside my body was really just a reflection of what was inside my body. The stars, the moon, and even the sun were all inside me. This is really what the Talmud is saying.

I had to think about that. There is really no difference between our sun and each one of the stars that we can see. From that I realized that our brain is located over the entire surface of our body. We think of our brain as being different from the rest of the body, but really it isn't. We are simply closer to our brain and that is why it seems so much larger. But if we see all of our cells as a network for our brain, then that makes a lot of sense to me. So our brain is the sun and each cell in our body is a star in the night sky. It is the moon which is the thing that is different.

For Jews, the moon represents the Jewish people. It waxes, it wanes, but it is always there. Jews base their calendar almost completely on the cycles of the moon. The sun plays only a very small part in how the Jews mark time and although we know how to use the Gregorian calendar as well as the next person, when we need to mark a very emotional date, we rely on the Jewish calendar much more than we do the Gregorian calendar.

I was four years old the first time that we landed on the moon, and for some reason, that landing made a huge impact on me. I followed all of the lunar landings faithfully. When I was a teacher, I always made sure to teach the story of how we landed on the moon—and I spent as much time on the intrigue surrounding the journey as I did on the actual landing. The journey to the moon was arduous. There was death and pain along the way, but it was a very important journey to make. And so I realize that the moon is our heart. Our heart will guide us accurately, but the journey to the heart will not be an easy one.

I have said before that everything is linked. How are the sun and the moon linked together? To answer that question we must return to mathematics. In our solar system, all of the planets orbit around the sun. However, they do not trace a circular path as they move around the sun—they trace an elliptical path. We are very familiar with circles. In a circle, every point is exactly the same distance from a single point. But in an ellipse, the path moves equally around two points. This is much more complicated. Again, it is no wonder we spend so much time confused here on Earth. We're busy searching for the ONE point, but we really have two. Where are these two points that help us to trace our elliptical path?

I mentioned before that I spent many years studying karate. Along with all of the typical katas and sparring, my school spent a lot of time studying street fighting. It was the perfect school for me. Whenever we would find ourselves in a difficult spot on "the street," my teacher would yell, "Use what's available, hit them where it counts." Hitting them "where it counts" meant one of three things. We were to hit them either on a Support, on the Solar plexus, or hit one of their Senses. Even the strongest attacker can be stopped by hitting any one of these points. The solar plexus is a spot where many nerves all come together. It is a very small spot, but it is completely unprotected—hitting someone squarely in the solar plexus will shut down their breathing. It is the name of this structure which is so interesting to me. The solar plexus—another name for this could be the sun point. But where would the moon point be?

I once had a friend who lived in Angel Fire, New Mexico. One time he told me a story about how he was driving on the road that runs from Angel Fire to the Vietnam Memorial. The road is in the beautiful valley of Angel Fire. The valley looks as if it had been carved by a glacier, but I'm not really sure if that is how it was formed. Keith was driving down the road, towards the memorial. The road is straight and is not very busy except for people traveling to and from the memorial. On this particular day, a helicopter crashed right in front of Keith. The crash was a fairly bad one, and although I'm not sure if anyone died, I know that everyone was hurt. Keith stopped his car and began rescuing the people. He was quite traumatized afterwards. He said that he felt immediately like he was back in Vietnam. He was pulling people out of a helicopter in 2005, but he really felt like he was pulling people out of a helicopter in 1974.

Inside our brain, we have a structure called the limbic system. Here, the emotions that we have experienced are stored. New experiences will sometimes cause those old emotions to come rushing out at us. This has nothing to do with time. I believe that the lunar plexus is the amygdala in the limbic system.

These two points are points of vulnerability for us. No matter how hard we try, we cannot protect ourselves at these two points. They are the points upon which all other movement rotates around.

How does all of this relate to the Layer of Stillness—the Layer of the Mind? All traditions speak of the need for calming the thoughts in order to better access the mind.

I like the explanation which says by calming the thoughts we are making our inner self like a reflecting pool. I always picture myself looking into a cirque and seeing the majestic mountains in the reflection. One time, when my kids were swimming, we all noticed how many waves were in the pool. The waves were high and choppy and all three of us wondered how it was possible that two small children could make such big waves. I know this explanation of stilling our deep waters is a good one, but I think there is more here.

I have said that our movement is elliptical and not circular. But the two shapes are really not so dissimilar. For that reason, I am now going to talk about a wheel and how its movement is important for us as we try to make contact with the Mind.

When a car is traveling down the road all four wheels are moving. What is really happening with the movement of the wheels? When I press on the gas of my car, the wheels begin to turn. If I'm driving on dry asphalt, my car will begin to move. However, if I'm driving on ice or snow, my wheels may begin to spin. How is the movement of these two scenarios different? On dry asphalt, the wheels are making good contact with the ground. If we were to calculate the velocity of each point around the wheel, we would see that the point of the wheel making perpendicular contact with the ground has no velocity—it is not moving. For me, this is an impossible fact to imagine—until I look at a wheel which is spinning in the snow or ice. In this scenario, it is very easy to see that all points of the wheel are in fact moving equally. There is no point which is making contact with the ground.

Often, if we feel we are not really moving in our lives we will use the saying "Spinning Our Wheels." We are speaking the truth here without even really knowing it. In order for the wheel to move a car—or a bicycle or even a unicycle—there must be a point of Stillness. Without it, no Movement is possible.

From here, we must return to the story of Creation. In the beginning, God created Breath, Light, Darkness and Movement. For six days, God created many things and on the seventh day, God did not create. I said before that Shabbat is a day of no Movement—no Change. And now I can see that with each week, we have a turning of the wheel. Shabbat is the point of the wheel making contact with the ground. Without such a point, no Movement is possible.

Here's how I see the real difference between what I am saying and what I have heard others say. In part I say this because I have had such difficulty remaining still in my life. It feels very odd to me to try and remain still. I find that I have no interest in it. But if I look at the wheel, everything makes sense to me. I can see that I need yoga to justify me—and put my edges back in order. By doing that my wheel can be in true—even my wheel that has two axles. I can bring my consciousness to a point, using my open places and that will bring me movement that is purposeful—my Mind will be the moving point that has no velocity.

Time and Change

Have you ever wondered why you wear seat belts in your car? The answer is simple really—rate of change. That's the easy answer, but only if you really understand what I'm saying. And once you understand what I'm saying you might see that wearing a seat belt in your car is one thing, but wearing a cosmic seat belt—the one you wear for security—might be something you want to leave behind you.

In all of my discussions, there is one thing I have left almost completely alone—Time. So, the question for this article is—how does Time relate to Change?

When I was a chemistry teacher my students were always trying to get me to blow up things. Their perennial request when they would walk into my classroom would be, "Can we blow something up today?" I would always answer, "No—I have other excitement in store for you."

There was one explosion that I sort of enjoyed however. At least it was the only one which didn't terrify me—exploding gas bubbles. These bubbles were fun. I would put a hose onto the end of a funnel and then connect the other end of the hose to the gas jet. I would then dip the wide end of the funnel into a mixture of dish soap and glycerin and turn on the gas. A perfect bubble would form on the end of the funnel, break off and then begin to rise towards the ceiling. My job would then be to take a lighted candle and touch it to the gas bubble. A loud bang and a ball of fire would cause my class to squeal with enjoyment.

Another demonstration which I absolutely loved, but which bored my class to tears was when I would place a lighted candle up at the front of the room and ask the students to tell me what was happening. I have tried this little demonstration with adults—in my home, when I am lighting Shabbos candles, and I get the same answer from them as I did from my students. "It's melting" is always the reply. Some students would even become angry when I pressed them—and I would have to concede that a small amount of wax does melt when you burn a candle, but what happens to the rest of the wax? Where does it go?

The answer to this question is very important to me. This is because burning a candle is essentially the same reaction as burning a forest or driving a car—and most importantly it is the same reaction which occurs within each of our cells on a daily basis.

Wax combines with oxygen to produce Water, Carbon Dioxide and energy when burned.

Gasoline combines with oxygen to produce Water, Carbon Dioxide and energy when burned.

Sugar combines with oxygen to produce Water, Carbon Dioxide and energy when burned.

One difference between all of these reactions is time—the one remaining thing which was created on the

First Day of Creation—and the one thing that I have not yet discussed.

Time is something that most people feel they understand very well. I would argue that we barely understand time at all, let alone the significance of it. Let's look more closely.

We all know that time moves differently depending on what is happening. It moves differently and yet it moves the same. If I am going to spend an hour in the dentist's chair and you are going to spend an hour doing asanas, my hour will move differently than your hour does—and yet, we can both agree to meet for lunch at the end of it and we will arrive to the restaurant at the same time.

I remember the day that Patañjali arrived in my home. I didn't realize at that moment that I had just welcomed Patañjali into my home, but looking back I can see that he arrived, fully formed, into my home some time during the winter of 2005.

During the time that art came exploding out of me, I began to carve soapstone. Carving soapstone is one of the most calming experiences I have ever had—except that it is hard on the hands. I found that my hands were always aching and I was forever cutting myself. I searched around for something that I could carve more easily and I found it. It is called Balsa Foam. After playing around with it for a while, I bought a huge block of professional grade Balsa Foam. The block was about two feet tall, three feet wide and three feet deep. The day that Patañjali arrived in my home was the day that huge block of Balsa Foam was delivered to my doorstep.

As soon as it arrived, I lugged it downstairs to my basement and it sat down there until I could figure out what to do with it. Whenever I carve something, I let the material speak to me. What is inside the material that needs to come out? How does the material call out to me? What is it saying?

That block of Balsa Foam began to talk to me. Not all of it—just some of it. The part that hasn't yet talked to me is still sitting in my basement, waiting. But as I listened, I realized that Patañjali was inside the block. Patañjali? Me? I've never done anything like this before. How do I start? So I just did what I have always done—I jumped in with both feet. I cut off a big slab of the Balsa Foam using my industrial "Tim the Toolman Taylor" saw, and I started carving.

I used an hobby knife to carve Patañjali. This is significant because yoga is our hobby knife. Patañjali arrived fully formed, but I needed Time and precision to see it. Little by little, over a period of about five months, I continued carving on Patañjali with my little hobby blade. Otherwise, I could have taken my industrial "Tim the Toolman Taylor" saw, cut off a chunk of the Balsa Foam and stuck the chunk upstairs in my bedroom. When you come to my house, I could take you upstairs to see Patañjali; although it might be difficult for you to recognize him since he would be covered with a very thick layer of Balsa Foam.

So with yoga we create space within us in a very precise manner—letting go of everything we don't need. I said before that creating Space helps to orient us, and here's why I said that.

When I started carving Patañjali I had to decide where to begin. As I looked at the block, I wondered whether I should begin at the bottom, at the top or somewhere in the middle. I decided to start at the bottom—contrary to how I usually do things.

I started carving Patañjali's snake and it went very well. I finished the snake portion of him with no difficulty. But then, I had to transition from the snake to Patañjali's torso, and I had huge troubles doing that. It seemed that no matter how much foam I cut away, Patañjali remained a block. I cut and cut and the more I cut the more disoriented I became. I was afraid of cutting away some of Patañjali's vital organs or one of his limbs simply because I couldn't tell where I was in his body.

Then, I took my girls up to the mountains. On the way up the mountain, I began to have trouble breathing. I thought nothing of it—we were only going up for the weekend, and I thought I would be OK. But the next morning I really couldn't breathe, and we ended up leaving early—right after lunch. And then I made a really huge mistake. I decided to take the girls to the hot springs before we headed down the mountain. But by then I really wasn't breathing. I became disoriented and I had trouble even making it back to our hotel. It was very difficult. Thank goodness for good friends who will drive long distances to help!

A couple of days later I went down to my basement and spent almost the entire day carving Patañjali—mostly because it was the only thing I could do. That was the day that I found Patañjali's torso. Suddenly it was there, right in front of me. I knew where I was—and I began to breathe.

It turns out that I was connected to that sculpture in ways I never would have imagined were possible. What was really happening was that I was down in my basement carving Patañjali, and Patañjali was carving me from the inside out. Remember I said that what I'm looking at on the outside is really a reflection of what is on the inside?

So I was trying to liberate Patañjali from the block on the outside, but what was really happening was that I was liberating myself from blocks on the inside. Blocks are thick and oppressive—and they hide things—which is why removing them helped me to orient myself in the sculpture. I had trouble feeling oriented every time I made a transition in the sculpture—torso to arms, snake heads to Patañjali's skull, etc.

Another word for transition is change. The subject of change is such a big one; it is not difficult to see why we have so much trouble with it. But looking at change from the vantage point of transitions gives us some new information. Initially when I was carving Patañjali, I was moving very quickly and easily. But then I almost stopped cold when I finished with the snake and started in on the torso. In physics, this phenomenon is called acceleration, which is how much an object changes its velocity in relation to time. If you'll remember, I began this article with a short discussion of rate of change and seat belts. This is the same thing. Let's look at acceleration a little more deeply.

Acceleration is simply a force. But what is a force? Webster's Ninth Collegiate Dictionary defines force as the cause of motion or change. But looking at force in a slightly different way shows us that another word for force could be strength, and that word brings us back to yoga. Yoga helps to make us strong enough to withstand change. However, there is still more to understand on this subject.

Let's return for a moment to Shabbat. You will remember that I said that Shabbat is a day with No Change. I also said that on Shabbat, the rabbis prohibited any activity which would have been necessary to build the

Temple. Another way to say that is—Shabbat is a day in which no Work is allowed. What is work?

Using mathematics, one can calculate work by measuring a force moving through a distance. This means if there is no movement, there is no work. I can stand all day long holding a heavy stack of books, and although I may become very fatigued, I am really not doing any work. Shabbat relates a lack of movement with a Holy Space of Time. When you think about it, Time is really all we have. I can lose my freedom, my body, my mind, but as long as I am breathing, I am subject to Time.

Relating Time to Work brings us to another mathematical concept. This is the concept of Power. Power is a measurement of how fast work is done. In other words, the quicker I can carry the books up two flights of stairs, the more powerful I am. There is another way of looking at Power however, and that is how quickly can I withstand change?

To understand that we can return to the seat belt analogy that I began with. We wear seat belts because they connect us to the car. In an accident, the car will come to a complete stop over a certain distance. The car travels through that distance in a certain length of time. If we can increase the distance that we need to stop, we can increase the time and decrease the power of the accident. However, if you're not wearing a seat belt, you will probably stop in the time it takes the windshield to stop. This will make the accident much more powerful. Looking at a seat belt in this way we can see that wearing one is a good idea in an accident, but I think that many people wear a sort of cosmic seat belt all of the time. This seat belt's effect is to slow the rate of change. But if change is the one constant in our lives, do we really need to slow it down?

I spoke before of the difference between a candle burning, gasoline burning and sugar (us) burning. I also said one big difference between these three very similar reactions is time. We are burning at a very controlled rate. Our temperature is a little less than 100° Fahrenheit, which is much less than the temperature at which a candle burns. We burn slowly, much as a candle burns slowly—but gasoline burns very quickly—in an explosive manner. Regardless of how fast the reaction happens, energy is liberated when the bond is broken in the molecule.

In any molecule, the atoms are held together by something called a bond. There are many ways of defining a bond, and I think nearly all of them are applicable. A chemical bond is a force, or an energy between two atoms which holds the atoms together. This bond, at least to my way of thinking, is very similar to a bond between two people. When two people have a bond, there is energy between them. It is that way with a chemical bond as well and breaking the bond liberates energy. We have seen this before. Remember the layers of the body? I said that the easiest place to see Light in the body was in the space between two neurons. But here, I'm saying that there is Light between two atoms as well. Breaking the bond (burning) liberates the Light—the Divine Sparks. Now that is interesting. But here is the really interesting thing.

One definition of yoga is to tie together—to yoke. Hmmm . . . that sounds like the definition of bond to me. Two or more parts uniting to become one. This is definitely a part of who we are, in the very smallest part of our being—the space between our atoms. No matter what we do, we will become ONE.

Time and Space

I put myself through college by working in a physics laboratory. The name of the lab was Condensed Matter Physics—but it really was a lab which dealt with the physics of light. My position in the lab was as an outsider—I was the only undergraduate student working there, I was one of only two women, and I was not a physicist—I was studying biology. My position as "outsider" allowed me to learn many things in that lab that I would not have learned had I been a conventional student.

I remember that somebody had a sign on their office door which said, "Heisenberg may have slept here." I have spent a lot of time thinking about that sign, and it is here that I begin this particular journey.

Heisenberg was a contemporary of Albert Einstein—and he even won an argument with Einstein about Time. Heisenberg is most famous for his Uncertainty Principle which states that you cannot know for certain an object's velocity and position at the same time. You can know either the velocity or the position, but not both. This seems fairly straightforward, but I assure you it is not. It relates two concepts—Time and Space.

When I started thinking about Heisenberg, I realized that of everything I have been discussing, Space is the one thing which was not created on the first day. This seems very significant to me, so I am going to pull on the thread and see where it leads me.

Years after Condensed Matter Physics, I worked in a chemistry lab, and I learned many things there as well. Looking back now, I realize that this lab was a chemistry of light lab—and so I will weave my two experiences together and see what happens.

At the chemistry lab, somebody else had a different sign on their door. This sign said, "Nature abhors a Vacuum." Aside from the obvious reference to housework, this sign made an impact on me because a large part of my job was to create a vacuum—and yes, it was a very difficult job. A vacuum is a Space—and it is devoid of anything else. This means that no gaseous molecules are allowed in a vacuum.

To do this, we would lower the temperature significantly—almost to the point where a molecule can no longer move. We would do this by first shrinking and then expanding the space. The point at which a molecule can no longer move is called Absolute Zero. There is no temperature colder than Absolute Zero—and this is because temperature is simply a measurement of how much a molecule is vibrating. Temperature measured from Absolute Zero uses the Kelvin scale. Water freezes at 273 Kelvin and boils at 373 Kelvin. To create the vacuum, we were working between 10 K and 4 K. That is pretty cold.

Going back to that vacuum sign, we can read it another way. "Nature abhors a Space." Aha! Now I know why creating space is such a difficult thing!

But why do yoga and Judaism talk about creating space? Are we really talking about the same thing or are two different things happening?

For a while I've had a theory that there are two main types of people—those that need to make space in their lives and those that need to claim their space. I've had this theory since taking yoga classes—and it is because I seem to have a knack for running into a certain type of person during yoga class. Every time I have taken a workshop from a senior teacher, I have had someone come up and steal my props. Each time, it has been a glaring, obvious example of someone trampling over my space. One time I was standing right next to my mat—and my mat was perpendicular to the wall. The woman whose mat was next to mine was also standing right beside her mat. We were standing waiting because the teacher had asked everyone to move their mats close to the wall—and we were already close to the wall. Another woman walked up to where we were standing, and in one absolutely smooth motion, grabbed both of our mats and threw them behind her. We were almost hit by our mats as they flew through the air. This utterly makes me laugh to think of it now, but at the time it made quite a different impression on me.

Scenarios like this have happened to me so often that I realized that these people were showing me something about myself. And they were showing me something about themselves as well.

Both types of people—those that need to make space and those that need to claim it—are living fear based lives. They are just using fear a little differently.

The people who need to create space are thinking that their center is in a spot where it really isn't. They think their center is somewhere different because a large portion of who they are remains in Darkness. These people are afraid of shining Light into the shadow aspects of themselves. As they move through their lives, they don't realize that they are whacking people or stepping on people with the parts of themselves that they can't see. Remember I talked about the paper cuts I received while justifying books? If a person is walking around with odd edges hanging out, they are apt to cut people with them as they walk by. These people are desperately trying to be smaller than they really are.

The other people are content to let their open places be constrictions. They are afraid to really open up and let themselves be seen. They think that it will be more painful to move into their open places than it will be to remain hidden. These people are also trying to be much smaller than they really are.

How does a person face their fear? The first thing for anybody to do is to go back to the river—back to the flow. Remember I said that Hebrew letters are a ladder to God? And remember I said that all one needs to do is to recite the alef-bet and God will do the rest? This is where you begin. It doesn't really matter if you begin with asanas, or Hebrew letters, but it does matter that you begin. And you need a bit of intention to face your fears. That's it! So it is really easy and really hard all at the same moment.

When I was born, my mother essentially squashed me flat. She did this by rejecting me. Parenthood was very difficult for my mother—I'm not sure she has ever loved me. I am sure that I was not an easy child. When I was four, I went to the hospital to have my tonsils out. In those days, you arrived at the hospital the night before the surgery. I remember sitting in the bed with the hospital pajamas on, eating dinner. As soon as I was done eating, I told my parents, "OK, you can go home now." My mother has complained to me my whole life that I don't need her—and it is true. The bond that should exist between my mother and I was broken long ago and I feel very little energy between us.

This does not mean that I have not maintained contact with my parents. Somehow I have always known that I would reach a point on my journey where I would need them. That point recently came.

Over my life I have shared very little personal information with my parents. I stopped showing them my grade reports in junior high, I have never talked about boyfriends or girlfriends with them and I have never spoken about my hopes and dreams with them. I have especially never let them see any of my vulnerabilities. But all that changed one day and there was nothing I could do about it.

One time my sister was in town with her husband and two children and I decided to have them and my parents over for a barbeque. I also invited a friend of mine as well as another family whose daughters are the same age as mine. I was in the kitchen, listening to everyone talk. And then I heard it—the question that changed my life. My dad asked my friend Steve, "How do you know Linda?" I began waving frantically at Steve, but he was enjoying the conversation with my dad, so he didn't notice my frantic waving. I heard Steve say to my dad, "From the Parkinson's support group." Oh dear. I heard my dad stumble, "Linda has Parkinson's?" By now Steve had seen my frantic waving, so he said to my dad, "Oh, no—she just enjoys going to the meetings to help out." But the cat was out of the bag. After a lifetime of knowing almost nothing about me, my parents had now been hit in the head with some very heavy information. Or so I thought. But the conversation just continued on—just as if Steve had never said anything about Parkinson's.

I tried desperately to get my parents to bring up the subject again. That night, I spent time alone with them in my garage while my dad was putting my mom into the car. I called them up the next day and invited myself over for dinner at their house. I even invited them over a couple of more times during the next week—all in an attempt to have my parents bring up the subject of Parkinson's. During this time I was so angry and hurt I couldn't see straight. My dad has never asked me how I am doing—never. I know he is capable of it though. When Ruth and I broke up—he called her and asked her how she was doing. To me, he accused me of taking the children from Ruth and said he couldn't believe how I was treating her. So I was waiting—much as I have waited all of my life—for my parents to show me some concern. And then it happened. On one of the nights I had invited them back over for dinner, we were sitting at the dining room table talking, and I accidentally brought up the subject of Ruth. My dad asked how her health was. I said, "Fine, Dad, she's on medication and it almost completely takes away her symptoms of arthritis." And my dad said, "How about you? What does your medication do?" It was over. I felt immediately transported into a different dimension—all with that one little question. The next day I called my dad up on the phone and thanked him for asking me about Parkinson's.

Everything is back to normal again—my parents make fun of me about how much I sleep—they think I'm lazy and klutzy, but I don't care. I'm no longer hiding myself from them. When they come over for dinner, I joke around with them, and tell them stories about my life. Twice now they have called me up—out of the blue—once to say they were bringing dinner over and another time to invite me out to eat with them.

The reason that I bring all of this up is that I faced my greatest fear. My mother frightened me more than any other person on this earth. By simply showing her who I was—mostly by showing her that I was vulnerable—I find that I no longer need to hide myself from anybody. I would highly recommend facing your fears to anyone.

Now I return to the definition of Space. It can be defined as Nothingness, or it can be defined mathematically—which is what Heisenberg was talking about in his Uncertainty Principle. Mathematically, Space is created by linking the axis of time with other axes of movement. I'll speak more of this in a moment, but I want to return to the subject of Space as devoid of anything.

I have been thinking about this since my daughter Lillian woke me up one Saturday morning by asking me if it was possible to breathe in space. I immediately knew that Lillian was asking about what I am writing about—even though consciously she knows nothing about what I am doing. But since then I have been watching events unfold—always searching for some reference to space—and several have come to me. It seems that while it is indeed difficult to breathe in space, when movement becomes possible, we begin to breathe again.

So then I go back to the Nature abhors a Vacuum sign and I look at the relationship between me and my parents. Even though it took over 40 years, there is no longer a vacuum between me and my parents. By definition, the temperature of any "true" vacuum should be Absolute Zero. No Movement Occurring. But, Nature abhors a Vacuum, and so, little by little, movement creeps into any situation, and with the movement, we begin to breathe.

Said another way, a vacuum is a space which is devoid of Light—and thus devoid of God. So it is no wonder that Nature abhors a vacuum and that little by little God will find ways to creep back in. Now I can see that we create Space in yoga in order to bring Light into places which have never had Light.

So now I return to the mathematical definition of Space—the one that says that Space is created when Time is linked with Movement. I think we've all heard about four dimensional space—with three of the axes typically labeled as X, Y and Z and the fourth axis labeled as Time.

One of my Chanukah menorahs has a phrase in Hebrew written on it. The phrase says, "*Nes gadol haya sham.*" This means "A great miracle happened there." Most people are at least somewhat familiar with this phrase even though they don't realize it. That is because most people have heard of the game *Dreidel*, where children spin a top and gamble with pennies depending on how the top lands. There are four Hebrew letters written on the dreidel but remembering what the letters stand for is easy. *Nun* means no pennies, *Gimel* means you get all the pennies, *Hey* means you get half and *Shin* means you put a penny in. My children love this game. I love it only if it is played with chocolate chips and not pennies.

I bring this up because there is a different phrase—one that you will find inside the State of Israel. This one says, "*Nes gadol haya po*", and means "A great miracle happened here." So children inside Israel get to play a slightly different game—I suppose those children with a dreidel landing on the letter *peh* become "*po*". Looking a little closer at these two phrases, we see that these two phrases link Time with Space.

In Judaism Holy Days do not last the same amount of time everywhere in the world. Inside Israel, Holy Days are shorter. For example, Rosh Hashanah is two days long outside of Israel, and only one day long inside Israel. Pesach is seven days long inside Israel and 8 days long outside Israel. This can all become very, very complicated. Looking at it without all of the details—we can see that there is a big difference between "there" and "here". The big difference is Time. Time is more accurate inside your Holy Space. This is also where you want to create Space—you don't need to bother about creating Space "there".

In my teachings about Fetal Alcohol Syndrome (FAS), I have spent a great deal of time teaching about Time. This is because people with FAS generally experience time differently than people without FAS. And the people without FAS seem to not be able to understand or accept this.

Typically, people in this society live in the past and in the future. Momentary excursions into present time are all people will allow themselves. In our heart of hearts, we think this is a good thing. We carry around our hurts and we spend our time preparing for the future. But kids with FAS live mainly in the present. They can't really remember what just happened and they don't really understand the concept of what is to come. I think they have a lot to teach people about Time. I don't look at either system as being superior to the other. I know that people who can't conceptualize the future spend a lot of time being anxious about very simple things. Instead, I think the ideal is a mixture of the two. Living in the present moment, being able to take information from the past and to understand that we are going somewhere we don't know anything about and which we cannot control is really the best way.

This is why we practice yoga. The linking of the different layers of the body can occur only in present time. Our constrictions are from the past and our open places will lead us to the future. We are participating in the act of creation if we allow these three to work in concert.

Chaos and Change

I can see that I am not done thinking about time. I suppose that is because I have so much of it right now. Not much else is going on in my life. I say that, and yet I really mean my outer life. My inner life is moving so quickly I almost can't keep up. But my outer life—nothing. What have I learned from all of this? Where is this nothingness taking me? To the first question I have many answers. To the second, I can only trust. Because there is a third question—how long can I live with an outer life that is Nothingness?

When I look back on my life, the last five years have been chaos. I can tell you society's definition of chaos—and I can tell you all about what society says you should do to eliminate chaos in your life. However, I have also noticed that the people who are telling me how to eliminate the chaos are people who have never been through it—not in any large sense anyway.

In any story, I like to start at the beginning. This story begins at the turn of the last century, with a scientist named Henri Poincaré who noticed that all phenomena are not predictable. If you spend even a minute thinking about that, you begin to realize that almost everything we believe about our World is mistaken.

I would like to spend some time talking about the significance of our lives and how I believe the Universe works. When I look at my life and at other people's lives, I see that we are desperately trying to control almost everything around us. I say almost everything, even though I haven't yet found something that we are not trying to control.

About four and a half years ago, I was sitting on the floor of my children's bathroom while they took a bath. The phone rang and I looked to see who was calling. It was the emergency room at Swedish Hospital. I didn't think too much of it at the time. But when I picked up the phone, there was the husband of my rabbi. "Sandy's had a stroke," he said and then he went on. "We're canceling all of her activities for the next week." I said, "Ben, I think you'll need to cancel them for longer than that." I said that, but I had no idea what that really meant, and I realized that Ben had no idea what he was saying either.

Change can happen so quickly that we have no idea what is really happening. Two years after the stroke, I think both Sandy and the larger congregation were still trying to deal with what was really happening with the stroke. As I say that, I also realize that what I really mean is that two years after the stroke, everyone was still trying to control the outcome.

Sandy was 34 years old when the stroke hit her. She was a very popular rabbi and it seemed that everyone in Denver knew and loved her. If there ever was a rabbi that could walk on water, Sandy was that rabbi. I became the public spokesperson so that the entire city of Denver would not bother Sandy or her family. I ended up having the same conversation with people over and over. "Sandy had a stroke? But she's so young! What caused the stroke?"

I realized very quickly that people were not asking about Sandy. They were asking about themselves. What they were really saying was, "What did Sandy do to bring the stroke on, and how can I keep that from happening in my own life?"

People tell me similar things about myself as well. I visited my karate teacher not too long ago. As we were catching up on each other's lives, I told her that I had Parkinson's—and she told me that her dad had just died from Parkinson's. Then she gave me her theory. She said that she believed that her dad had Parkinson's because he hadn't drunk enough water in his life—he had essentially desiccated his brain. She said that she had completely changed her outlook on this and now she was furiously trying to undo any damage that she may have done by not drinking enough water. She showed me her huge water bottle that she now carries around.

This theory is so absurd that it makes me laugh—except that she wanted me to come back and study with her—essentially give her lots of money so that she could work with me. I don't think so.

I can't speak about Sandy's stroke, but I can speak about me and Parkinson's. Parkinson's is a disease of the Space between two neurons. Basically with Parkinson's I have fallen into that Space. That to me makes much more sense than that I didn't drink enough water.

If you'll notice, I have never said why I think I have Parkinson's. That is because I really don't care. I have looked back over my writings, and I see that I do sometimes ask a Why question. "Why do I breathe?" "Why do I feel differently after yoga than I do after soccer?" "Why is Change so hard?" These questions seem fundamentally different than "Why do I have Parkinson's?"

Does there really have to be a reason why I have Parkinson's?

Henri Poincaré was one of the first scientists to describe chaos theory. Basically he said that there really doesn't have to be a reason why—and the more time we spend looking for the reason why, the more time we are throwing to the wind. What Henri Poincaré said may seem straightforward, but really what he said was and is such a huge change to the way we have constructed our lives, that over a hundred years later, we are still struggling to understand the significance.

Think about it and you will know it is true. All of science is based on the ability to look at something and predict something about it. Poincaré said that you can look at something, but you won't be able to see everything you need to see, and the something you can't see could very well be the thing that explodes out of control. Said a different way, small differences which either you can't see or don't notice, can multiply upon themselves and create a system that is wildly different from anything you could have imagined.

Looking at the world before Henri Poincaré, we can see a long history of what is now called Determinism. Sometime in the 1600's, Isaac Newton was sitting under his apple tree when he realized some very important information about gravity. He also was able to describe how planets orbit around the sun, and science was turned on its ear by the possibility of prediction. The inter-weaving of early Greek (Aristotle) thoughts on the predictability of nature combined with scientific thought on the same subject has greatly shaped who we are today. We believe that everything that happens in our lives has a precedent with something that happened in the past.

In ancient Greek mythology, chaos was a wide open Space. Another way to describe this could be a gaping hole. The important thing here is that for the Greeks, out of chaos springs creativity. I think we have seen this before. Remember the wheel turning, with the perpendicular point having no velocity? This idea of chaos seems to be the same thing, only on a bigger scale. I said at the beginning that chaos feels very much like nothingness, and it is one of the most uncomfortable feelings I have ever known. For almost 5 years I have felt doors and opportunities closing down right before me. In my head I have a picture of a funnel, and I am dropping down through that funnel. Luckily a funnel has a single solitary hole at the bottom of it. I believe I am to be shot through that hole. I say believe, but I really mean trust. After five years of nothing really working out, I can no longer say that I believe, only that I still trust.

Before I move away from chaos, there are a couple of more things I want to say. I have used mathematical and mythological means to define chaos, but I haven't used the common definition of chaos—until now. Looking at myself, I can see how the common definition of chaos fits neatly with the other two. Mathematically, chaos is an inability to predict outcomes; mythologically, chaos is a big hole and commonly we speak of chaos as disorder.

When I look back over the last five years I can see that I have desperately been trying to maintain order in my life—with varying degrees of success. One of my most glaring examples came when I began dating a woman some time last year. As soon as I started seeing her, my life completely blew up—time-wise. It was as if I had stepped into quicksand. I have never had huge troubles arriving to places on time—some people have even called me habitually punctual—but I was completely the opposite during the time I was dating Rosa. I could arrive somewhere hours late—where did the time go? I was late for everything during this time—even taking my kids to school. Eventually I realized that I wasn't supposed to be dating Rosa, and when I realized that and corrected the situation, time began flowing normally for me again.

Explained through the lens of chaos, what was happening was that little changes in myself that I hadn't really noticed were multiplying upon themselves, and changing my life in ways I had no way of predicting—or controlling. The harder I tried to arrive somewhere on time, the more late I was. I also see something else happening here though. I believe that when we step into chaos, we are stepping into a place where time is no longer linked to movement in the way that it was before—hence the feeling of disorder. Entering into a period of chaos is very important, although it is not very easy. But you don't want to control the chaos—you want to ride it out—to get through it as quickly and as easily as possible.

Let's go back to the wheel theory one more time. I said before that chaos is the grand wheel—bigger than *šavasana* or meditation or Shabbat. When you look at all of the points on the wheel, the one that has the most force on it is indeed the point with no velocity. So as you are riding the chaos wheel, when you feel the most squished is really when you are at that bottom point on the wheel. Recognizing this can greatly help with the terror of being on the chaos wheel. You will get through to the other side—but only if you stay right where you are.

Pain

In all the time I played soccer, I only remember the faces of three opponents. Two of the faces that I remember were on the same team. I remember both of those women because I had occasion to experience them as habitually unsportsmanlike. The third woman I remember because she fell on me—and injured me. When I worked at Condensed Matter Physics, we all decided that it would be fun to play on a co-ed recreational soccer league. The players on our team were all physicists and all worked either in the Gamow Tower or at JILA. The only two people on our team who had ever played soccer before were me, and a post doc from Tunisia named Mohammed. I loved Mohammed. He was a big man with a big personality. If Mohammed was around, you knew it. Mohammed and I were team captains.

On this particular day, we were playing some other team of beginners. Maybe they were from IBM or something, I don't know. I remember the ball was very far away from me when the person who was guarding me stepped on my foot and then fell. She was a very tall woman—and very skinny—and when she fell, it was sort of slow motion, but it carried a lot of force. She fell sideways right onto my knee. I both heard and felt the crack when she hit my knee and I fell down. I remember sitting on the ground for a little while, and Mohammed was yelling in the distance, "Shake it off Linda." I shook my head at him and walked off the field. Mohammed gave me a few minutes to pull myself back together and then said, "You're going back out there." I walked around for a bit and I decided that my knee didn't feel right—it felt as if it could bend forwards as easily as it could bend backwards. I considered going back out to play, and then I told Mohammed I just didn't feel like playing any more.

What had happened? I had blown my knee out when that woman fell on me. I've seen other people blow their knees out and I can tell you I've never seen anyone just get up and walk off the field. I had something similar happen to me almost exactly eight years ago.

One day the garage door opener was not working properly so I unhooked the door and raised it up by hand. Ruth and her mother were in one car with the two kids and I was in another car because I was going to get my hair done. We both backed our cars out of the garage and then I went to close the garage door, but my hand slipped and one of my fingers got caught in between two of the door panels as it was closing. I had to work hard and fast to stop the garage door from continuing to close because it was quickly cutting my finger completely off. If the door had moved another centimeter, I would have lost the end of my finger. I moved the garage door back in the opposite direction and extracted my now very thin finger.

I remember cussing a lot after this happened. I couldn't believe how close I had come to losing my finger and it scared me. I looked into Ruth's car and I saw both her and her mother looking at me with open mouths. I thought Ruth's mother was upset because I was cussing so much. I finished closing the garage door, waved to Ruth and her mom, and I drove away.

As I drove away, I looked more closely at my finger. It was dead. I looked at it and thought, "This is what I will look like when I'm dead." I didn't want my finger to be dead, so I began to squeeze it, hoping to bring some blood back into it. The squeezing helped, and I went to my hair appointment and never mentioned a thing.

I remember going to karate, and having my teacher comment on my finger. But all she said was that she could see that I had hurt it, so I didn't give it much thought. A couple of weeks later however, when my finger felt no better, I finally went to the doctor. He said it was broken. Oh, well, I could definitely see how that happened, although it never dawned on me that I could have actually injured my finger. He set the finger and I wore a splint to karate that night. My karate teacher said that she could see that I had broken my finger weeks before, why hadn't I realized it?

Why indeed? Why do I have an inability to feel pain? But is that what is really happening, and why is pain such an important thing to feel?

My yoga teacher Jayne has my number. She knows that I don't feel pain the way other people do, and she calls me on it. If I feel pain in her class and I don't tell her about it, I am in big trouble. This has been particularly helpful to me. I have come to see that I don't have to live in pain—that it is actually possible to move out of the pain. I have seen something else as well.

I recently realized that it is not that I don't feel pain; it is just that I have a much larger pain that drowns everything else out. This pain is so large and so painful, that I barely notice any other pain because everything else is so minimal in comparison.

If I sit quietly, and listen to what my body is telling me, I see that I have a huge hole in the middle of me. It feels and looks to me like someone took a 45 caliber gun and shot me right through the middle at close range. I have had this pain with me ever since I was a little girl and I remember when I first decided to ignore it. I remember deciding that I was going to live a "good life." This one little decision completely changed my life, but can I continue to ignore that pain?

I think not. This leaves me with a dilemma however. I'm not sure how to get rid of the pain, and I'm not sure how to move out of it without simply ignoring it. I also can't fill that hole up with something else—I've tried and it just doesn't work. Being angry about the hole doesn't work either—I've tried that as well.

Before I do anything with this pain, I feel I should look at what yoga says about pain. In the first article, I said there were 5 layers in our body. These were:

1. Physical body
2. Breath
3. Light
4. Movement
5. Stillness

Which is the layer of Pain? It is the layer of Light—the layer of communication. Hmmm . . . so pain is a communication. I looked up the definition of pain in <u>Webster's 11th Collegiate Dictionary</u> and written there was the following:

A basic bodily sensation induced by a noxious stimulus, received by naked nerve endings, characterized by physical discomfort and typically leading to evasive action.

The last part of that definition really makes me laugh. "Typically leading to evasive action" is exactly what I have done in my life. But does it get us anywhere to evade pain? If we do that, we are essentially ignoring the message. So we must do the opposite of evasive action—we must embrace our pain.

A man named Martin Buber, who died the year after I was born, wrote a book that has changed Judaism. The book is I and Thou and basically, the book says that there is a big difference between experiencing something and having a relationship. Buber said that having a relationship is where a person will encounter God. In having an experience, a person will only be able to encounter an object.

There is an inherent difficulty in describing Martin Buber. I find this most clearly in the statement, "The Tao that can be described is not the real Tao." Buber would say, "The Thou that can be described is not the real Thou." Hmmm . . . of course I'm going to go ahead and try to explain it anyway!

I said before that our constricting experiences shape us and propel us to move. If I sit inside the big hole in the middle of me, I find that I feel like a big doughnut. But if I look more carefully, I see that it isn't a doughnut—it is more like a lifesaver. Well that is interesting. It has always felt like the opposite of lifesaving to me. But maybe that is because I have always been experiencing the big hole—not having a relationship with it.

Interestingly enough, I find that if I sit inside the big hole, it is not painful. The pain comes only when I am outside of it, looking in. What is happening here? Going back to the definition of pain, I see that pain is caused by naked nerve endings. Maybe that hole is just big enough to fit me. Maybe the hole exists because I was ripped out of myself. Maybe when I sit inside the hole, I am no longer a doughnut or a lifesaver—I am a sphere—perfectly formed and in unity once again. The pain is gone because the nerve endings are no longer naked—they are completely attached and I am once again in relationship with Myself.

I can say this another way. Nes Gadol Haya Sham—and—Nes Gadol Haya Po. Both sayings are equally true—but if I'm standing on the outside looking in, it sure is a lot more painful. If I am experiencing myself, I see myself as an object, but by moving into my Sacred Space, I am able to have a relationship with myself, and there's nothing painful about that at all.

I can see this same thing happening with the smaller pains that I feel in yoga class. In small steps, Jayne has taught me to embrace my pain—simply by telling her about it. And because our constricting experiences force us to move—by embracing our pains, we are able to move into our open places—once again becoming the moving point that has no velocity.

Love

M y entire life people have been telling me that I am a fighter and I know they are right. Not only am I a fighter, I am a very good fighter. But looking back over my life I can see a pattern in the things I have chosen to fight. I have been fighting being human. I have to say that I have found this whole business of being human pretty painful. Sometimes it seems like I simply move from one painful experience to another. But now that I am looking at Martin Buber, I can see that all the pain is because I have been having the experience of being human. Finally, I am ready to have a relationship with my humanity.

For a while now I have felt that both yoga and Judaism are simply here to help us be human— fully human. In many respects, being fully human is my definition of Unity. Another way to say this is when a person is fully human they are enlightened. To be sure, having the experience of being human is not necessarily a bad thing. There are many things I have seen and learned in all my experiences. It is just that now I am ready to unify my experiences into a whole.

I have spoken about many things—mainly God, the structure of our universe and how we fit into that structure; but in looking at my life, I know that I have only talked about part of the story. In order to understand this business of being human, I need to understand one final thing—Love.

What do yoga and Judaism have to say about love? I may be missing the boat here, but I don't see either yoga or Judaism spending a lot of time on the subject of Love. This seems odd to me—mostly because I have always seen Love as a sort of power cord—a way to plug into The Source. Without Love we remain separate, adrift and unable to be fully human. Why is this? What is Love?

In science, there is an idea of something being so fundamental to our existence that we are unable to properly define it. Some of the things which fit into this category are Time, Space, and Mass. I would put Love into this category as well, as I believe that for most people Love is so fundamental that they do not question its existence or importance.

Some time ago, I was a substitute teacher at a K-8 school in the Denver metro area. At this school I was a special education teacher and my job was to go into classrooms and assist the special education students. Several of my students were emotionally disturbed, four seriously so. I watched these students carefully during my time at the school and I spoke with the classroom teachers about them. I mentioned to the teachers that I think these children have experienced some serious abuse and they agreed with me. But life for these children continued as if nothing bad was happening to them. This left me with the feeling that I mentioned to the teachers that these children were bleeding all over the carpet and they just said back to me, "Yes, but they need to learn mathematics so they can be productive adults." How can the children learn mathematics if they are bleeding all over the carpet?

Shouldn't we attend to the bleeding first? But nobody seemed too concerned—they told me that, "We just hope they'll make it through."

Well I can tell you that we simply cannot let people go through life without being hooked into a source of Love. And before I go on let me be very clear. The problems I saw in this school are societal problems—certainly common worldwide. It is not the fault of these teachers that they are not seeing these children's problems as life threatening. Indeed, the world is content to let people live without Love.

What is Love? To answer that question I return to the story of tsimtsum—when God withdrew in order to create the universe. With God's initial out—breath, Light was created. Thus, the world is made of Light. Previously in these articles I have referred to Light mainly as something we can see. But Light is more than just what we can see. I once heard someone define a spectrum as "that with no end and no beginning." I'm not sure that definition is specific enough for science, but for us that definition will work just fine. So Light is a spectrum and it is really energy; different types of Light have different amounts of energy. This means that Love is really just like Light.

If you go to your stove and put your hand just above the burner you will be able to feel if the burner is hot or not. This ability to feel heat at a distance is due to Light—we would say that it is due to infrared Light. Love is also something that we feel, and so I would say that Love corresponds closely with infrared radiation.

Regardless of what we eat, we are really eating the energy from the sun. It is the same with Love. All sources of Love come from God. When a baby is born, the parents hold the baby, provide for his needs, and love the baby.

The baby, in turn, is like a little seed, and grows in the Light of Love. I was once at a luncheon, honoring the former Cherokee Head Chief Wilma Mankiller where I heard a reference to this that made a lot of sense to me. The audience was asking Chief Mankiller her opinion on different issues and somebody stood up and put their arms out as if to cradle a baby and then said that, "A baby is planted into our arms as a tree is planted into the soil." Wow. That made a big impression on me. The previous generation is the foundation for the next. A child's arms do not reach back towards the parents, they reach towards the future. But what happens when a child has no one to hold her?

We know exactly what happens when a child has no one to hold him. When I was the coordinator for the children's diagnostic clinic we once saw a boy who had spent three years in a Romanian orphanage. His mother was wanting clarification on whether or not this boy had autism. I don't remember what the diagnosis turned out to be, but I do remember that this boy was profoundly affected by his time in the orphanage. He did not hold eye contact with people, did not search out people when he needed comfort and did not know how to interact with his peers at school. This boy's mother was trying everything to help her son out, and I applaud her efforts. But will this boy ever be able to feel his mother's love?

To answer that question we must go back to mathematics. Remember I said that we are really ellipses, and that our two essential focal points are the solar plexus and the amygdala inside the limbic system? I gave one definition of an ellipse, saying that all parts of the ellipse move equally around these two points. But there is a second definition of an ellipse, one that has importance here. An ellipse is shaped such that shining light onto one of the foci will cause the light rays to be reflected onto the other focus point. Essentially we all are a satellite dish that is calibrated to receive and transmit Love.

I looked up satellite dishes on Wikipedia and written there was the following:

> A parabola may also be characterized as a conic section with an eccentricity of 1. As a consequence of this, all parabolas are similar. A parabola can also be obtained as the limit of a sequence of ellipses where one focus is kept fixed as the other is allowed to move arbitrarily far away in one direction. In this sense, a parabola may be considered an ellipse that has one focus at infinity.

Hmmm . . . That is very interesting. This is exactly what I am saying. By receiving Love from our parents (or others acting as parents) we are in essence set up to receive and transmit God's Love. But, if we are born into circumstances where that Love is sporadic or non-existent, our satellite dishes do not get set up to receive Love. So the question then becomes can we give Love at a later date and hope that satellite dish system will kick in? I think we can, and although it may never function like it should, even receiving a faint signal of Love is better than receiving none.

The next question I want to answer is: Why is Love so important?

Receiving God's Love is what makes us human. This is more complicated than it sounds, so I will explain a little more. I know for certain that each of us comes to this world with certain gifts—certain parts of ourselves that are already integrated. But each of us also comes into this world needing to integrate other parts of ourselves. We need God's Love to define the areas that we need to integrate. Otherwise these areas remain forgotten to us. So instead of being like a deliciously solid piece of Gouda cheese, we can end up being more like a piece of Swiss cheese: still delicious, but with many holes. For these people, the task of becoming fully human is impossible—and yet we just keep living our lives as if nothing is really happening. But when you open yourself up to these people, you see that the pain of humanity is absolutely unbearable. So what can we do about it?

It is here that I find yoga and Judaism to be the most helpful. The principle of ahimsa states that in order to truly be non-violent, each of us must search for the areas of violence that we hold within ourselves and let them go before we can ever hope to diminish outward violence. Judaism says this another way. Rabbi Hillel said, "that which is hateful to you do not do to your neighbor." Another quote of Hillel's seems to take this a step further. "If I am not for myself, then who will be for me? And if I am only for myself, then what am I? And if not now, when?"

So we begin our journey with ourselves, knowing that it will ultimately help others. We identify the sources of violence that we carry within our being, and then let go of that violence, knowing that we will then be able to search out the sources of violence in our outer world. This is very important because the opposite of Love is not Hate, it is Indifference (Elie Weisel). We must not remain indifferent to the pain and suffering of others. We must be active in order to participate in the process of Creation. For Jews, this is known as Tikkun Olam—Repairing the World.

Inertia and Habits

When I was in college I had a favorite physics professor. His name was John Taylor and he had a profound impact on my life. In speaking with other people who also took physics with Dr. Taylor, I know that he had an equally profound experience on many, many people.

Dr. Taylor was from England. I loved just sitting in his class and listening to his accent even though I couldn't always understand him. One time I was in his office getting help with homework and he started talking about something I could only understand as a "garraige" (rhymes with carriage.) I was on my way home before I realized that he had been talking about a garage. Dr. Taylor had a lot of energy and spent most of his time running around the lecture hall. In many ways, he brought physics to life for me. Quite often I would take something I learned in his class and run downstairs to the Condensed Matter Physics labs and ask the graduate students to discuss this new piece of information with me.

I bring up Dr. Taylor because I want to talk about one of his demonstrations. He had a little circular table that he had covered with a very pretty tablecloth. On the table he had placed a very nice glass vase with a single place setting. He walked up to the table, imitating a maitre d' and in one smooth motion pulled the tablecloth right off the little table. I closed my eyes, expecting a huge crash and broken glass everywhere, but there was no sound. I opened my eyes and there was Dr. Taylor, standing there holding the tablecloth—the glass vase and the single place setting were sitting on the table, exactly like they had been before. Wow. This made a huge impact on me—so big I went home and tried the same thing—only at my house, the glass vase and the single place setting ended up on the floor.

What was happening with Dr. Taylor's little demonstration? I've already made reference to it in a previous article—inertia. Inertia is the reason we must wear seat belts in a car. As we are traveling along in the car, we will stay in motion at whatever velocity we were traveling at—until we are acted upon by another force. Inertia also works for objects at rest—those objects will remain at rest until acted upon by another force. So what happened with Dr. Taylor's practiced hand was that he was able to yank that little tablecloth out from under the objects so quickly that they didn't really even "notice" the tablecloth had vanished.

How does the concept of inertia relate to yoga and how can we apply what we've learned into our daily lives?

Inertia manifests itself as habits. My life tends to remain the same until some outside force comes along and changes it. In yoga, we look at the habits that we bring to certain poses. How do I hold my midsection and lower back when I am standing? Do I "stick" my butt out behind me, or do I keep it tucked under me? Do I slump when I am standing or do I raise my sternum and keep my shoulders back? We often have to notice a habit before we are able to change it. Yoga brings awareness to all areas of the body so that we are able to look at our habits honestly—and then we can see how it might be possible to change them. Sometimes even though we may see something that we want to change, we may not have the flexibility or the strength to bring about the desired changes at that moment.

This is all intertwined with *ahimsa*. If I go through my yoga practice labeling all of my habits as "bad", then I am practicing a subtle or not so subtle form of aggression against myself. If instead, I simply notice where I am placing my body in space—my body will tell me the message that is waiting for me. Sometimes the message is simply that nobody has ever pointed out a different way to be before. Other times, the message is that I am losing contact with the autonomic nervous system in my body. In that case, how much damage am I causing to myself if I get angry that I have to once again remind myself to stand up straight and breathe?

Sometimes, even if a particular habit is not due to a disease like Parkinson's, it can be especially difficult to change. In karate class, my teacher used to go around the room yelling, "It's not your Be-hind! It's your Be-under!" We would all put our consciousness into that part of our body, noticing if we were the ones she was talking to. I found that I was almost always the one she was talking to. But now I laugh every time I find myself sticking my butt out behind me. I've been practicing karate for years, and now yoga, and I still have trouble not sticking my butt out behind me. Sometimes I think I must be the world's slowest learner. But then I go back to my karate teacher yelling about it in class and I just laugh.

So that is well and good for yoga practice. But how does this all relate to the world-at-large?

I have noticed that there are many problems in the world. When I look a little closer at these problems I can see that they are caused mainly by habits. This is just the way things are. When I talk to people about these problems, the response is quite often, "Well, you know everything is perfect. Nothing happens without a reason." Quite often these people then launch into a discussion about how I'm trying to change things I really shouldn't be changing—because after all, that's the way things are.

But remember I said that what we see outside ourselves is just a reflection of what is happening inside ourselves? Well, the reverse is also true. And so we can say that inertia in our society manifests as habits. Looking at this through the perspective of yoga, we can also see that once we have identified a habit, we can listen to what that habit is telling us and then we can make a decision whether we want to change that habit or not.

Let me give you an example. When I first began teaching, I was hired in an inner-city high school in Denver. I was hired to teach math and science in the bilingual program. When I got to school, I found that I was a teacher of "untouchables." And as a teacher of untouchable students, I myself became an untouchable.

That first year I taught earth science, biology, algebra 1 and algebra 2. Four preps and six classes. That is a lot for any new teacher you might say, and you would be right. But on top of the four preps and six classes I had five different classrooms, located on three different floors and on opposite sides of the building. I used to sprint between classes. I still remember sprinting down the hall and just as I got to the teacher's lounge the door opened and out stepped a para named Miguel. I knocked him flat and all of the papers he was carrying were scattered far and wide.

But none of what I have described to you mattered very much to me. What mattered to me was that I was not a member of the science department. I taught biology and earth science and yet I had no access to anything the school had to offer in the way of materials to teach earth science and biology. I didn't even really have text books. I had nothing. So how was I supposed to teach anything?

I spoke with many people about this, and everyone's reactions were the same. "You're in the bilingual department. What do you expect?"—How is the science department supposed to open itself up to you?"—This is just the way it is and you're not going to change it."

Hmmm . . . When I said I was a fighter and that I was a good fighter I meant it. I began arriving at the high school early in the morning—before any of the science teachers got there. It took me a couple of days to find out how early to get there. I would wait patiently in the hallway every morning. Usually it was my ex-partner Ruth who would come first. Of course she wasn't my ex-partner Ruth in those days; she was just the first teacher to arrive in the mornings. Every morning, without fail, I would be there waiting for her. And every morning I would ask her to let me into the stock rooms. Now there are a lot of stock rooms in a high school. Some mornings I would need into the biology stock room and some mornings into the physics stock room. Some mornings I would need into both. This continued day after day.

At Christmas time that first year, I received an invitation to the science department's party. I forced myself to go, even though I was terrified. Making headway into the department was one thing, and if I'm talking about teaching science I can talk with anybody. But at a science department party I'm going to have to make small talk and I hate that. However, I knew that I had won the battle with that invitation so I forced myself to go.

Second semester was the same story. I was very patient that year. Towards the end of the year, I noticed that Ruth was coming around—finding me in one of my many classrooms and we were spending time talking together. At some point I asked her for a key to the storage rooms and she agreed. I don't think she exactly realized it, but as soon as she gave me that key, I was a full-fledged member of the science department. And at the end of the year, Ruth asked if I wanted to be roommates. Well, you know how that story ended, and as a result of my trying to become a member of the science department, I ended up bringing two of the most beautiful people (my daughters) I know into my life. I know that Ruth feels the same way.

I could tell you about other injustices I have seen and how I have "fought" my way through them. Many of them are similar stories. In junior high I had a gym teacher who would leave the girls in the basketball courts to throw a tennis ball against the wall and would then take the boys out to the fields to play baseball. You can imagine that as someone who was actively squashing all of her femininity, the last place I wanted to be was with a bunch of girls for 50 minutes with nothing to do but talk. Every day I would meet the gym teacher, and I would tell him that, "You can't just leave us over there by ourselves! We deserve a gym class! This is unjust!" Every day, the same thing, over and over. At the end of the first semester, guess what? The girls were allowed to play with the boys.

So, when I identify a habit in our society that is in desperate need of changing, I find that I am loathe to simply accept that the system is the way it is, that it is perfect and I am not going to be able to change anything. Let me tell you how I would change things.

For this part of the story I return to the K-8 school that I was subbing in. Remember the kids that I say were disturbed? Well my opinion on that is that if you're in MY school, then the second you step inside the doors, you are going to find love. I would hire a pair of teachers—one would be a woman who knows how to love—an Earth Mother of sorts. This person would have a satellite dish system the size of Texas. The other person would be a really physical man—someone who both knows how to love and how to physically reach people. This team of teachers would take these kids and teach them all sorts of things. They would be outside learning how to play kickball and watching insects; they would be inside learning music and arts. They would prepare lunch together and then they would go outside and play at recess together. As the kids got the idea of love, they could begin spending some time together with their class—the class they're in now. Little by little, they would begin to integrate themselves into the world.

Do I know if this system would work? Absolutely not. But I know it's worth a try, because I know the system we have now doesn't work at all. And because I know about inertia, I also know that if I don't do something about it, the situation may very well continue on and on and on.

Perfection

There is a prayer which is comforting to many people. The prayer is as follows:

> God, give us grace to accept with serenity the things that cannot be changed, courage to change the things that should be changed, and the wisdom to distinguish the one from the other.

> Reinhold Niebuhr

The teachings of this prayer are much more difficult than many people think. Gaining the wisdom to tell the difference between something that I can change and something that I cannot is essential and at the same time very difficult. I believe many people confuse the two categories. They spend their time trying to change the things they cannot and they pray for the serenity to accept the things that they really could change. I can give an easy example.

I have Parkinson's. I can't change that. I can, however, change how I relate to Parkinson's.

I am speaking of being a victim. I can choose to be a "victim" of Parkinson's or I can continue living my life—pursuing my sacred path. There is no doubt—my sacred path took a bit of a turn when I began experiencing the symptoms of Parkinson's. Things that I have always been able to do easily became very difficult. Jobs that I might have pursued are no longer available to me and it is the same with certain activities that I really enjoyed. But when I thought about my difficulties, I realized they had absolutely nothing to do with pursuing my sacred path. True, I can no longer play soccer, I have trouble making it through a full day of work and my body hurts a lot more than it used to. But when I really think about it, Parkinson's does not affect my ability to become ONE. Wow. That made a huge impact on me. Parkinson's puts a limit on what I can do in the exterior world, but it doesn't change what I can achieve with my interior world.

Now I have to watch myself. How am I feeling? Have I taken my medicine? What will I be doing later on in the day that I need to prepare myself for now? These questions are always present in me, and if I forget to ask myself one of these questions my life becomes a lot more difficult. But if I keep these questions in mind, my limitations with Parkinson's allow me to do more, not less. This may seem confusing, but remember I am not talking about the exterior world—and from everything I've seen about this world, what I am saying holds true for most people and for most limitations.

Last summer I took my girls on a camping trip with three other families. Between us we had ten children and we took up two large campsites. For nearly the entire trip the rain was relentless and by the third day of sleeping in a wet sleeping bag, I wanted to go home. Not only that, but there was a yoga workshop back down in Denver that I wanted to go to. So on Wednesday we all began packing up. Now packing up four families' junk is very difficult, especially when one of the women in the group really likes shopping—even when she is camping. We had much more stuff leaving than we did coming. I could feel that I was getting tired, but if I stopped working, then I might miss the yoga workshop, and really I was so sick of the rain that I was ready to scream. So I kept going.

Now you have to picture what I looked like. I had on my daughter's pink poncho, with the hood of the poncho under my baseball cap. The poncho was too small for me, but was the best rain protection I had that day. I gathered up all of the trash from our site and began lugging the trash sack to the dumpster, which was several campsites away. Needless to say the trash sack was very heavy, and I could only carry it by swinging it with one leg and then taking a step. It was a slow process, made even slower by my increasing symptoms of Parkinson's due to the fact that I was working past my stopping point. At a nearby campsite my movement slowed to almost nothing. By an unlucky coincidence, I was right at a large RV's campsite and the RV was completely filled with people. I continued my journey. Suddenly I heard the RV erupt in laughter and I looked up and I could see all of the people inside the RV pointing at me and laughing. Now I forgot that I was wearing a silly hat and an even sillier poncho. I tried hurrying, but to no avail. All that I could think was to yell at the people, "What are you laughing at? You're in a rented RV!" When I got back to our campsite, one of my friends put everything into perspective. She said, "Well, you do look pretty silly."

Throughout these articles I have tried to bring both the world-at-large and my own personal life to my yoga mat. If I can understand what it is that I am really doing on my yoga mat then yoga can transform my life. Previously I talked about how yoga is our knife that we use to cut away those things which we don't need. There is a strong element of honesty here. If I am "leaning" on something that is false, then continuing to "lean" on that something does not serve me. In fact, it is a form of ahimsa to do so. In yoga we will often use props to maintain the integrity of the pose. The props enable us to move beyond our usual way of doing the pose. We lean on the prop and not on something false. Another way to say this is the props help us with our limitations. Those students who refuse to acknowledge their limitations end up not progressing in their yoga. So I must acknowledge my limitations to maintain integrity in my life. If I don't, then I will end up perpetually in front of a rented RV full of people who are laughing at me, unable to move because I haven't taken care of myself.

And even though I'm using a big example here—remember that I am talking about any limitation. Other limitations that I have in my life are having hip problems, wearing glasses and being easily bored.

What I am talking about is related to perfection. People want to be "perfect". They want their days to go perfectly, they want to sit in the perfect seat at a restaurant eating perfect food and they want to have a perfect job. But we don't really spend any time looking at what perfection means, and besides, wanting to be perfect, and actually being perfect are two completely different things. Quite often when something like a bad disease or a job loss hits us we spend our time being angry because we think we can no longer pursue a "perfect" life.

It would be most helpful to look at perfection for a minute. My Webster's dictionary says that the word perfect means to faithfully reproduce the original. Hmmm ... that is very interesting. If we can realize our Divine nature, we will be going a long way to perfection. This sounds a lot like the word Namaste to me—the traditional greeting where my Divine nature recognizes your Divine nature.

There's another definition of perfect in my Webster's dictionary which says that the word perfect comes from the past participle of the Latin word to carry out, or in other words, to thoroughly make. So there it is—the concept of perfection is really a concept of creating. Put these two meanings together and we can see that our job is to use our divine nature to create.

Our notion of perfection causes huge problems for us in our everyday lives. People often say that God is perfect, and then they somehow wrap a lot of shame and guilt around themselves. They also say that God is unchanging and this is somehow connected to this concept of perfection. But God has never been static for me. And when I look at stories that are told about God, the stories are never about God not changing. The stories are always about God being a dynamic presence in the world, and in people's lives. At the very least, as a person changes their relationship with God changes. When I look at human beings, the same cannot always be said. As I change, you may not be able to see the changes and instead treat me as you did in the past. It seems most helpful to relate to God as a constant presence in my life, not as someone who doesn't change.

One other thought on perfection from my Webster's dictionary: it means complete. The word Shalom, which means peace in English, comes from the root word for complete (in Hebrew). So to be perfect means to be complete, and this brings us back to Union, or One. So yes, God is perfect—and at peace. Rather than think of God as unchanging, you could think of God as Stillness. At first glance, this concept of God as Stillness seems to contradict my earlier explanation of God as a dynamic process. But then look at the wheel, which is turning and which has the point of stillness at the bottom, and you see that God is both a dynamic process and a point of stillness. I used to think that change and movement were the same, but now I realize that movement results when the process of change is combined with a point of stillness.

As I look at all of this I see that it is no wonder we spend so much time being confused. I feel as if we are all playing the game "Pin the tail on the donkey." We're being spun around and around and then our task is to find out precisely where we are, but by then we're dizzy and disoriented. We probably should all say the Serenity Prayer by Reinhold Niebuhr for good measure.

God, give us grace to accept with serenity the things that cannot be changed, courage to change the things that should be changed, and the wisdom to distinguish the one from the other.

Patañjali

I n the last article I related the concept of perfection with the concept of creating, but then I find myself asking the question, "What are we trying to create?" The answer to this question is not as straightforward as it may seem, so I will pull on the thread and see where it takes me.

In yoga one sees a lot of people trying to be perfect. I suppose this behavior is everywhere, but on the yoga mat is it blatantly obvious. I've seen people get angry when they can't do a pose—and the difficulty of the pose doesn't matter. One time I was in a class that was doing *matsyendrasana*, which is a very complicated pose. To describe the pose for the layperson, I would say matsyendrasana is a pretzel pose. I frankly couldn't believe the teacher was asking us to do what she was asking us to do and it was making me laugh. I had so much fun during that pose. But then afterwards the teacher asked us how we were feeling. One woman said, "humbled;" another said, "angry"; and so on.

I remember that day very well. The woman who said she was humbled by the pose really caught my attention. She has trouble with almost all of the poses; what made her think she could do a really difficult pose without any struggles? And then I realized that the woman made a big impression on me because I am so hard on myself in other areas of my life.

So what is happening here and how can yoga help?

We look to Patañjali, the Father of Yoga for help with this question. Patañjali has four hands. The two inner hands are in namaste and the two outer hands are holding objects. Patañjali's right hand holds a disc and his left hand holds a conch. The disc is the Sun and represents the Source; it is Divine Light and it is also our own inner light. The conch is a container of life. Walk along the beach, pick up a conch and hold it to your ear. We say it is the ocean we are listening to, but you could also say it is your inner self. In addition, a conch can be used for communication, simply by blowing on it. It is important to realize that a conch is grown by an animal, and when that animal either grows too large or dies, it will leave the conch behind and another animal—one who is growing larger—will come to inhabit it. Looking at the conch in this way, I see that it represents our human nature, our legacy and our connection to other human beings.

The disc and the conch both represent Space. The conch can easily be thought of as a space but the disc is too. Mathematically a disc is the area inside a circle. And a disc can either be closed or open, depending if the actual line demarcating the circle is included or not. That, of course bears discussion at a later point, but for now we will just say that our goal is to create space on both sides—Divine and Human. This means that our goal is to make our Divine Nature more apparent and to increase our capacity for life.

Earlier I said that "perfection" is really obvious on the yoga mat. Another way to say the same thing is to say that some people who study yoga have really big egos. For our purposes here, ego and Ego are two separate things; Ego being your sense of Self.

What does a big ego look like? At some level, it is being way too hard on yourself. At another, it is being way too hard on other people. At yet another it is trying to seem like you're "bigger" than you really are. I have seen all of this in the yoga community—people getting angry with themselves, teachers treating others below them badly when they think nobody else is watching and students asking incessant questions which are designed to show off their knowledge.

Yoga helps a person to create space. But WHERE the person creates space is up to them. It is really easy to use yoga to blow up your defense mechanism—sort of form a big balloon around you. The problem here is that if you blow up a big balloon around you, then you are kept inside the balloon and your sense of self (Ego) is very small.

It is much harder in yoga to create space by emptying yourself out. One can understand just how much more difficult this is when you realize that by emptying yourself out you have to "kill" certain other parts of yourself. Sometimes the parts that you must "kill" may be those parts which kept you safe through your childhood or they could be the parts which give you status in society. It's different for everybody, but for everyone it is the parts you identify with the most.

When I was walking along the beach in Mexico the night that I realized we all have the sun and moon inside of us, I saw something else as well. When I looked at the sky I could see stars, but I couldn't see very many stars right over the cities. Looking down the beach at Playa del Carmen I saw a haze of light right over the city and the same thing was in the sky over Cozumel and Cancun too. I realized that we use light to hide things from ourselves and others. By letting go of what we don't need (thoughts, beliefs, patterns) we are shutting off our light pollution—essentially making our inner self absolutely clear. The goal is to have a night sky like the one you see in the mountains. There, the sheer number of stars is absolutely stunning.

Yoga can help you turn off the light pollution—empty your cup of light pollution. Picture your sense of self as a cup and the contents of the cup as your ego. If your cup is full of light pollution, then your sense of self is full of ego and there is no room for anything else to come in. You are in danger of hurting people without realizing it because the light pollution keeps you from seeing clearly. Also, if you increase your ego too much, the light pollution will begin to spill over the top of the cup. I imagine this looks like a Halloween cauldron, with carbon dioxide spilling over the top. This is another way to describe the balloon that I was talking about earlier. I like the cauldron image as much as the balloon image because carbon dioxide is a poison to us. If you somehow manage to take in a breath full of carbon dioxide (I used to work in a brewery), it will feel very much like a train is being rammed up your nose.

When a person manages to empty their cup, they have a very strong sense of self—a very healthy Ego. These people are not hard on themselves, they do not treat the people below them badly and they do not try to show off in front of other people. If they do, they see it and they make repairs. When the Bible speaks about "my cup runneth over," it was not talking about light pollution. It was talking about a cup that was full of the Divine and the Providence that comes from being in contact with the Divine.

And that is why we empty the cup—to fill the cup with Divine Light, Divine Purpose. The person with a strong sense of self can be of service to others because the ego is not sitting there getting in the way. This is what Patañjali is showing us. Two of the arms hold the conch and disc and then the other two arms show him bringing the two into contact. This is how we can use our Divine Nature to create, how we can become whole, at peace and perfect. It is indeed the only way to become perfectly human.

Barriers

As I look at meaningful movement I can see that I need to understand one more area—that of barriers. The way I see it barriers are beliefs we hold. These beliefs are invisible to the person holding them, but they make the person's world very small. Barriers are internal—unlike obstacles—which are external and which provide the means for our purposeful movement. At first glance barriers seem insidious; so it is important to see how they work.

Barriers are easiest to see when looking at someone else's. Recently I was a long term substitute teacher. I taught reading and writing to 6th graders. I taught 6th graders once before and I remember them as being squirrelly but fairly easy to manage. I would count time off, "All right class, that's 5 seconds, that's 10," and I would put check marks on the blackboard. My class would immediately quiet down. It was relentless, but easy enough. These 6th graders were different. I'm not sure I ever really got them to quiet down and I was shocked at how mean they were to one another.

Then one day the principal came over the loud speaker and told the kids they were NOT to leave school for any reason that day. It was the day of the immigration rally being held in downtown Denver. Historically all of the schools in the metro area experience a student walk-out on the day of the rally. I spoke with my students about the immigration policy, the rally and what the rally was asking people to do.

I was somewhat surprised to find out that my students did not believe they had a voice in this country. They believed that no matter what they did, nobody would listen to them and nothing would ever change. This hit me hard because I could see their belief seemed very real to them, but was not true in any objective sense.

I began to wonder about these types of beliefs because we all have them inside of us. These beliefs feel like barriers to me—and at first glance they seem insurmountable. But are they? And what can we learn from our barriers?

When I examine the barriers I carry around inside me, the one I can see is that I have always believed that I do not make an impact on those around me. Looking back, I can see how I have hurt people with this mistaken notion. Over time, I have learned to act as if I am impacting others. By acting as if I make an impact, I have been able to see that indeed I really do affect others.

There are people who have helped me see this. When I did my student teaching, my cooperating teachers sat me down and told me that classroom management would work smoothly if I had a relationship with EACH student. They told me to hold a personal conversation with every student every week. The conversation did not have to be lengthy, but it couldn't have anything to do with school. They wanted me to make a list of each student so that I didn't forget anyone. This little piece of information transformed my life. Not only were they right, it did make classroom management really easy. I was forced to concede that having a relationship with me was important to my students.

I took this advice into other parts of my life as well. I spoke briefly of the stroke that my rabbi had when she was 34 years old but I didn't mention that I was the president of the synagogue at the time. When she had the stroke the entire congregation was absolutely bereft. I began talking to each person I saw at the synagogue. I kept a list of the people I spoke with and remembered who I needed to talk to. I found I could do this because I was president. I used the role of president to be able to have an impact on people. As time went on, I became somewhat of a celebrity. I would be standing in line at the supermarket and the person behind me would ask, "Aren't you the president of that little synagogue?" I thought that people were only interested in me because I was the president. But someone finally mentioned to me that it really wasn't because I was president that people wanted to talk to me—they wanted to talk with me because I was Linda. This was very important for me to hear, although it was very hard for me to accept.

As I look at these stories about my barriers, I see that without the help of my cooperating teachers and my good friends at the synagogue, I would still be unaware that anything was amiss. To me, the way I was seemed perfectly natural. But even with the help of my friends, it took me over ten years to really make a dent in this barrier.

I can see something happening here. When I had the belief that my actions did not make an impact my interior space was small. To me it felt cozy and safe. As I began to work with my mistaken notion, the barrier was moved further and further away—and my interior space grew.

Now it feels more like a temporary wall—the kind at a synagogue or church which can be folded up to create a large social hall.

Barriers have the potential to increase our capacity for life. Moving around our internal walls creates internal space. We can also see this by looking at our sense of survival—the thing that each of us bases our security on. Most people base their sense of security on financial issues. Removing financial security can really frighten people and they begin to act as if they are dying. Lifeguards at a swimming pool are taught to let a person begin sinking before jumping in to save them. If a lifeguard jumps in too soon, the person is likely to attack them from the sheer terror of drowning.

I know from my own experience that this is how I react when my sense of security is threatened. I also know that just because I am feeling like I am dying; it does not mean that I am really going to die. By reminding myself of this, I can begin to act as if I am not dying and hopefully I will not attack the people around me.

Let's return to the idea of barriers as interior walls. When you are in a room, there are six walls around you. One to your left, one to your right, one in front of you, one behind you—and then two more—above and below you. This common sense of security that we all feel is like the floor and from time to time our floor drops out from beneath us, leaving us dangling in thin air. It does this to remind us that we really are safe. We are part of a grand plan and everything will work out.

This leaves me with a final question. How can yoga help to identify and remove these mistaken notions?

My experience with yoga teachers is that they point things out about me that I would not be able to see otherwise. One of these things is that I am an "over-achiever." At first it may seem odd that being an over-achiever would be a barrier—after all, in American society we like over-achievers. But there is no room on the yoga mat for an over-achiever, and I am grateful to my yoga teachers for pointing it out to me.

As far as I can see, another barrier we all hold is that at one time or another we think we can't do something that really we can. This seems to happen on a daily basis for me in yoga. But by working with this every day, I have begun to see that it just isn't true—and I need to remain open to the possibility that indeed I can do it.

One other way yoga can help is by doing the same pose in different orientations. For example, *dandasana*, *adho muka svasana*, *viparita karani*, *ardha halasana* and handstand against the wall at 90° are all essentially the same pose. Yet when I am doing each pose, they all feel completely different. Some are hard, some are easy and one can be frightening to me—the handstand one—and yet, at their core, they are all the same pose.

Now when I am doing any one of these poses I go back to *dandasana* and see what I need to do with my body. I know that even though my body feels really different in each pose, it is not. This is particularly helpful when I am afraid. Even though I am terrified, I need to know who I am and where I am. In this way I can keep from hurting someone—and I can also keep from hurting myself. And each time I look a barrier squarely in the face, I practice moving around my interior walls—which increases my internal capacity for life.

Healing

Patañjali is the Father of Yoga because he compiled the oral teachings of yoga into a discreet set of writings called The Yoga Sutras. This act changed yoga forever and is the reason we are now able to study yoga 2200 years after Patañjali lived.

Sutra means thread and each Yoga Sutra is a simple sentence outlining what must be done in order to achieve Samadhi or wholeness. One interesting thing here is that we use the word sutra in English every time we say the word suture. A suture is also a thread and it is a specific type of thread. A suture ties together things that are alive. By this I mean if you have a wound, then you could use a suture to tie the wound together. We also have sutures in our head—where the plates of our skull fused together after our head was finished growing. So I look at the Yoga Sutras in the same way. They are threads that tie together the different parts of Life. Remember when I said that the word ONE is the unification of two or more parts? This is what the Yoga Sutras are—instructions for unifying your many parts into a whole.

There are many stories which are told about Patañjali and I love all of them. I love the stories because we can have a relationship with Patañjali through the stories and also because the stories tell the "truth" about Patañjali much more than historical facts can.

One of these stories is about his mother, who had a lot of knowledge about yoga but no one to pass the knowledge on to. She desperately wanted a son to teach yoga to, so she went down to the water and prayed to God. While she was praying she scooped up some water into her hands and just as she was about to throw the water back, as a sort of offering for her prayers, she looked down into her cupped hands. Swimming around in the water was a serpent. She looked at the serpent for a while and as she looked, the serpent changed into being part human. The little person looked up at her and asked, "Will you be my mother?" And even though I am sure that she had never in her wildest dreams imagined this type of an heir, she said yes. She then transmitted all of her knowledge to Patañjali and it is this knowledge which he wrote down in the yoga sutras.

There is another story which talks about Adisesa, a serpent god who is an incarnation of Vishnu. Adisesa found Gonika, Patañjali's mother because Adisesa wanted to bring yoga to humanity and he was impressed with her knowledge and devotion. This story is important because it shows us where Patañjali comes from. Patañjali is an incarnation of one of the Gods of the Hindu Trinity—the Sustainer Vishnu.

The Hindu Trinity or Trimurti consists of a Creator, a Sustainer and a Destroyer. The three are linked as ONE because Change is a process and in order to create, something else must first be destroyed. As I see it, for Hindis, God is a process.

Originally I spoke about <u>The Tibetan Book of Yoga</u>. The book describes the beginning of life as the initial in-breath and the end of life as the final out-breath, and then a space in between the in-breath and the out-breath. I related this to a tombstone and said that the entirety of our lives is represented by the dash between the two dates on a tombstone. If we look at that dash in a slightly different way we see that the dash links the moment of birth with the moment of death. When I look at the Hindu Trimurti I see that the Sustainer Vishnu is the link between the Creator Brahma and the Destroyer Siva in exactly the same way. This may not be as straightforward as I think it is so I am going to explain a little more.

From a western perspective it is easy to see the moment of creation and the moment of destruction as Change. However, I have always looked at the middle part as a desperate attempt to keep things the way they are. Now I realize that I was completely wrong. The Sustainer Vishnu's role is as much Change as either the Creator or the Destroyer's.

This is significant because yoga comes from Vishnu by way of Patañjali and Adisesa. Since everything is linked and it is the linking which is key, this means that yoga is a link in exactly the same way Vishnu is a link and in exactly the same way that breathing is a link. This needs a little further explanation.

- ´ Breath links the layer of the Body with the layer of Light
- Breath links Darkness and Light
- Movement links Darkness and Light
- Our life links the first in-breath with the final out-breath
- Vishnu links Brahma with Siva

- The present moment links the past with the future
- The present moment links our constrictions with our open places

I see now that I could go on and on about links, but I want to look at yoga and the first thing I see is that yoga is present time so it links the past with the future, just as the breath does. I can also say that yoga is the link between our constrictions and our open places and also that it is the link between the Body and the Soul. Yoga links the human and the divine and at another level yoga is the link between Samsara and Samadhi. I have the very real sensation that I am switching words around but I'm really talking about the same thing over and over. I'm talking about Change—I'm talking about God.

Change is the foundation of the universe. I have looked at change in a number of ways in these articles, but I can see one more way that I want to look at Change—I think that Patañjali has something more to say on the subject.

Patañjali is a snake. He is part human too, but he never stops being a snake. The entire lower portion of his body is a coiled snake, which represents potential. The coiled snake then moves into Patañjali's body at the base of his spine and continues traveling up his back until the base of his skull. Anyone who has felt kundalini energy knows that the potential of the snake is capable of traveling up and down the spine. And then the snake comes outward again, forming the hood and heads of the cobra above Patañjali's head. Because the snake plays such a role in the representation of Patañjali, it is important to know what snakes represent.

Linda A. Roe

A snake sheds its skin, and it does so with its eyes wide open. The skin is shed in one big piece. We can say that the snake leaves behind what it no longer needs and because of this it represents transformation or change. And by coincidence or not, we look at change in almost exactly the same way we look at snakes. Change is out there, waiting to "get" us, and when it "gets" us it will be very painful and we may not be able to survive. I also know from experience that when we come upon snakes it is usually by surprise, and that is the same way we see Change sneaking up on us.

But for all the bad feelings, snakes are beautiful. When I was a kid my grandparents had a nest of snakes living beneath their front porch. Looking back now I am laughing at my grandparents. They are just about the only people I know in the world who would allow a bunch of snakes to live below their front porch. The snakes were a beautiful iridescent green and I absolutely loved them. I got bitten by one of the snakes after my brother pulled on its tail, but it didn't bother me—I still absolutely loved those snakes.

I must confess that I now harbor some fear of snakes. This happened because years later I was hiking with my dog when we came upon a snake—only this time it wasn't a garter snake—it was a rattlesnake. The rattlesnake bit my dog. Everybody lived through the experience, but I confess to being afraid of snakes to this day.

I've had more contact with snakes over my life, but I only want to tell one more story about them. At the high school where I first began teaching, I spent one Friday afternoon chatting with Ruth and another teacher named Gary. Gary loved snakes and had a couple of them at school. While we were chatting Gary had one of the snakes out loose in the room. Suddenly we all realized that it was late, and we went to put the snake back in its cage so we could go home. However, the snake was wrapped tightly around one of the legs of a chair. We tried to pry the snake from the chair leg, but the snake didn't want to move. Clearly we were not in control of the snake—not even a little bit. To this day I'm not sure how Gary ever got home because Ruth and I ended up leaving before he managed to get the snake off the chair.

This story is very significant as we look at Change. Sometimes I know I have tried to "hurry" change along. But if it is not time for change to leave, then it's not leaving. This remains one of the most difficult aspects of Change for me to accept. If I want something to end, then Change has to be in agreement or it won't end. If I want something to begin, then Change has to be in agreement or it won't begin.

Surprisingly enough, the medical community uses the snake to represent itself. The medical community sees the snake as a healer, mostly because it leaves behind what it no longer needs. Looking at snakes as healers I see another link. The snake links Purposeful Change with Healing. This means that whenever you are experiencing Change you are experiencing Healing. This is a very important way to look at Change.

There is one other thing I want to look at and then I'm done.

In asana yoga one of the foundational poses is *tadasana*. This pose can be found in all other poses. The other foundational pose is *šavasana*. I have often wondered why tadasana and šavasana are foundational poses and now I have an answer. Tadasana is mountain pose. Mountains are formed from tremendous change—indeed by the cataclysmic collision of two tectonic plates. But look at how beautiful mountains are—and how strong. This means that we must connect with change in our poses—and I'm not talking about the parts of the body which move—no. We must connect with the process of change. How is it that we should embrace change? By knowing who we are and where we are—and we do that by locating our sacrum, rotating our shoulders, etc. Then, the other part of the foundation of asana yoga is šavasana, which is the still point. As we remember, the still point is what allows us to make meaningful movement—otherwise we are simply "spinning our wheels."

What is it exactly that I am saying? I think I can describe it most easily by going back to the image of me making plastic wrap in chemistry class. There were three layers there—two distinct layers of chemicals and then a third layer separating the other two. This third layer is dynamic. The more contact, the more of a reaction. If too much movement comes to this dynamic third layer, then the whole thing will become an unusable goop, but if a glass rod is drawn from the bottom layer to the top, then a useful reaction will occur in that third layer.

This is why we do yoga. We make sure that we are not turbulent in our layers, especially the layers of movement and stillness. Then when we do a pose—say *pinch mayurasana*, we bring some of the first layer into contact with some of the second layer. When we do pinch mayurasana we need to find both tadasana and šavasana. Tadasana helps us locate each layer; the pose is the glass rod (the link) and where the layers react, that is the point of stillness—the moving point that has no velocity—it is the šavasana pose.

Yoga is a vehicle for this process. But all roads lead to the Divine and as we've seen, breathing, time, and indeed even living all will take us through this process. Another way to say this is that we experience God when we breathe, when we're experiencing time and when we're doing yoga. Everything is God; there is nothing that is not God.

Bibliography

Webster's Ninth New Collegiate Dictionary. Springfield, Massachusetts: Merriam-Webster Inc., 1983.

Roach, Michael. The Tibetan Book of Yoga.New York: Doubleday, 2003.

Scherman, Rabbi Nosson, et al., ed. The Stone Edition Tanach.Brooklyn: Mesorah Publications, Ltd., 2000.